Dedicated to all the men and women who wear and have worn the uniform, and to the family members who wait and have waited for their return home.

ASHAU VALLEY, 1968

Clawing up the abyss of unconsciousness; as the heat and stench of urine and feces from voided bowels Dance Macabre with the ghastly aromas of hot copper and iron and cordite and steel from explosives – from my blood – from the blood of the dead Team Leader whose decapitated chest cavity I'm covered with. Now the first sick stirrings of pain and nausea as my brain reels from sensory overload.......LAY DOG!! NO SOUND........NO MOVEMENT!! ....My mind scrambling in desperation, attempting to still the rush of adrenaline and heartbeat hammering so loud it will be my own suicide call to the murdering Demons from the North, briefly glimpsed by one cracked glance from a swollen, bloodshot, blood drenched eye barely able to focus past concussion shock.

Enemy Warriors feeding my horror and fear, circling around us like two-legged vultures stabbing and shooting anyone or anything that moves. Anticipating the bayonet, the bullet, I still freeze even as sharp steel begins a slow and vicious probe with casual malignancy. Sudden rage and anger......as I refuse to die today. Lord Buddha smiles......briefly......the Gods of War nod......and suddenly, Iron Dragons fly to me spitting lead death at my tormentors. Alternate waves of relief and agony wash over my torn flesh and raw, exposed nerves as Screaming Eagles and Golden Black Horsemen pull me from the Pit of Doom, All the Way to the grotesque insanity of Now.

Stephen J. Jacobs
U.S Army/RVN 1968-1969

Contents

The Veterans

The Family of Veterans

The Contributors

Editor's note

When I thought of facilitating writing workshops, one for veterans and one for the family of veterans that would culminate in an anthology and a formal reading for the community, I had no idea where it would lead, or even if it would work. I'm happy to say, this project has been more meaningful, and more successful than I could have imagined.

As the writing workshops progressed, I witnessed the veteran participants search with courage for the story they wanted to write. I witnessed their voices emerge as they wrote their stories and memoirs. I witnessed the family member participants delve into philosophical dialogue about war and their relationship to the military. All the while, we supported and encouraged each other to keep going, to keep exploring and discovering our truth, our story. And above all, to keep writing no matter how daunting it seemed. Most of these stories were difficult to write, but important to write so we could embrace what needed to be embraced, and in the process, share with others what we needed to share. And we listened to each other, knowing that when we listen to another's story, we share in their journey home. With each interaction, the bonds between us deepened, becoming something special to carry within our hearts long after the project's end. It is my hope that each of us learned a little bit more about ourselves as a person, as a veteran or a family member, and as a writer.

This project would not have been possible without the following individuals and organizations in their support and belief that writing and storytelling helps heal the wounds of war and empowers veterans and the families of veterans: Wellness Works, Glendale, especially Kathy, Lisa, Rachel, Teri and everyone who smiled and said hello; The Los Angeles County Arts Commission, and The Los Angeles County Board of Supervisors, notably The Honorable Hilda L. Solis of District 1, and The Honorable Kathryn Barger of District 5; Poets and Writers, West, and Jamie Fitzgerald and Brandi Spaethe for their continual belief in this work; Janice Shyer,

Sandra Squire Fluck, Justine Helena Bugaj, Chuck Smallwood, Dallas Dorsett Mathers, Stephen J. Jacobs, and Terre Fallon Lindseth, Studio 44, G-force Grips, No Ho Copy, Mil-Tree, Returning Soldiers Speak, The Deadly Writers Platoon, and a special shout out to Kenneth James for his endurance as a proofreader, and his ability to find the typos that slipped by me. And the thank yous would not be complete without acknowledging the adroit editing and proofreading skills of Lucy, Wes, Adam and Rick who spent another day going through the draft with me one more time!

It is my honor and privilege to have been a part of this worthy and meaningful project. With respect and much love, thank you, my dear veterans and family members for this journey of writing and exploring and discovering what it means for me to be the daughter of a veteran.

Leilani Squire

THE VETERANS

The Two Times I Turned Twenty-One

Wes Cloys

Grow up. Act your age. Be responsible. Show maturity.

I don't know who came up with the number 21. At one time your twenty-first birthday marked the end of adolescence. It was a milestone to mark a period when one should be grown up.

Over fifty-five years ago, I reached my 16th birthday. Sixteen was a big deal in the early sixties. It meant you were old enough to drive, and having a driver's license meant freedom and responsibilities.

Two short years later—my 18th birthday. More responsibility. Register with the Selective Service Board. (Selective ... I wonder what that means?) It means some mature person is being responsible for some young person's life.

When I turned 18, I was far from being an adult. An eighteen year old boy, in the state of California could not be married until he reached the age of twenty-one without having his parents' permission. That law would eventually change, and I'm sure being married helped some guys from going into the military. I knew that there was no way that I was going to ask my parents if I could get married. That would be real responsibility.

Anyway, in 1963, I turned 18 in a small Kansas town. Hays, Kansas to be exact. I understand it is a growing city some fifty years later. I was responsible because a few days after my eighteenth birthday, I went to the local post office and registered for the military draft with the Selective Service Board. They made it convenient for you. You could register at any post office. Eventually, my records were transferred to my home location in Pasadena, California.

Now that I am 18, I can do some things on my own. Like buy *Playboy* magazines or cigarettes. I've only bought a few packs of cigarettes in my lifetime, which would amount to about five U.S. dollars. Then, a pack of cigarettes was twenty-five cents a pack. I think that included the tax. America was great. As for the *Playboy* magazine, I read most of the article and barely remember Miss July 1963. Carrie Enwright. She was one of "The girls of summer."

That was the last summer of innocence. No, not my innocence. The nation's innocence.

That summer, I was starting to be responsible and trying to act my age. Is that even possible? Now, I still wasn't mature. I would be 23 the first time I would be eligible to vote for the President of the United State. (A history note: at that time you had to be twenty-one years old to vote.) So I didn't need to worry about being too responsible. Another great time in America.

I was, however, mature enough to join the military without my parents' permission. So this is what I did—maybe not being too responsible—I joined the Army in January of 1964. Perhaps I was feeling more mature and trying to act my age.

After basic training I was stationed at Ft. Belvior, Virginia, which is a short distance from the nation's capitol, Washington, D.C. It was during the time of President Johnson's Equal Rights Movement. Because there was civil unrest, there were many public demon- strations during that time in Washington, and parts of my weekends were spent on stand-by for crowd control. Now I felt like I was acting responsible.

I also was fortunate to be able to spend my nineteenth birthday (that fell on a Father's Day evening) with some civilian friends. We were like kids acting their age, not having to be serious. The times, they were changing.

Just seven months prior to this, the President of the United States had been assassinated. The nation's capitol was the center of change. There were racial tensions; equal rights issues and talk of war in a far off land. The summer of 1964—the age of innocence—had passed.

It had been two years since being at home with my dad on Father's Day. My next assignment was Ft. Lewis in the state of Washington. I was the youngest member of the platoon I was assigned to. Most of the men in my platoon were twenty-one years old or older. Some of them were college graduates, but most of them were draftees, meaning they had grown up enough to be a mature adult who was responsible for their life. Or at least they had two years trying to be responsible.

One Saturday, shortly after being in the platoon, the guys asked if I wanted to go to Seattle that evening with them. As I remember, it was a three-hour drive north on old Highway U.S. 99. (There weren't any freeways then).

We arrived in Seattle around 10:PM. I had been to Seattle before, but this time, we went to the Playboy Club. Now, I had driven past the Playboy Club in Los Angeles before. This was not Los Angeles. This was a small nightclub with the Playboy theme. The waitresses were dressed in the traditional Bunny outfits. They seemed extremely friendly, attractive and professional. This is the observa-tion of a first time nineteen year old.

There were seven of us and I'm quite sure that six of us had been there before. Drinks were ordered, and I never having the opportunity to order a drink before (and trying not to act my age) and being responsible, I ordered a Rum and Cola. I remembered a song, something about drinking rum and cola.

It was an uneventful, but fun evening. The hours seemed to pass quickly and it was sometime past midnight when we started back to Ft. Lewis. The guys were harassing me about only having two drinks. That is when I told them that I was only nineteen.

These were great guys. I'll always remember them. They were from Oklahoma, New York City, Wisconsin, Detroit and two of them were from the state of Washington. They laughed at the nineteen year old, handed me the keys to the car and at 2:AM, on Sunday morning, I was designated return driver. That was showing some maturity.

I remember the car being big, maybe a 1962 or '63 Oldsmobile or Buick. Four guys in the back and three of us up front—without seatbelts. They helped me find Highway 99 South, and from there I was on my own. They then passed out, and I drove south. We arrived back at the base early Sunday morning before breakfast. We sat around the mess hall drinking coffee and having some good conversations. I was beginning to feel mature.

Two weeks later, the guys asked me if I wanted to go to Seattle again. I said okay. This time, I was dropped off at the Denny's coffee shop in downtown Seattle around 10:PM. They told me they would pick me up some time after 1:AM. I spent the time walking around town, and then I went back to Denny's.

I had a few cups of coffee. I can't remember if it was Seattle's best or not. Oh, and I did order a pie a la mode. I also met a waitress. She was three years older than I was.

The guys came to Denny's, had some coffee and around 2:AM directed me to Hwy 99 South, and soon I was driving the big boat with six passed out short-timers dreaming of being civilians with

Playboy bunnies. As I drove the old highway passing small motels, all night coffee shops and gas stations, I thought I could stay on Hwy 99 right into Los Angeles. But it was just a dream. America was great.

One weekday at noon, soon after the last Seattle trip, one of the guys told me to go to company headquarters and see the company clerk. I went to the office and checked in with the clerk. He said there were some papers for me to sign. He said they were routine, and he was in a hurry, so sign the documents and get to lunch. Of course the company commander wasn't in the building. I was being responsible. I signed the papers.

At noon, almost two weeks later, I returned to the company commander's office. The Captain wasn't there but the clerk was. Again, he was in a hurry and said, "Sign this form and this is yours." I did as he told me to do, and then he handed me my new military I.D. Card. The documents that I had previously signed were forms reporting a lost I.D. Card. I had no idea that I was getting a new card. My original card was still in my wallet.

The new card had my birthday—June 15th. Okay, that is correct, but the year stated 1943. So that means that even though I was actually only 19, I was now 21. It was the first time I turned 21. My good responsible, mature buddies didn't want to spend their last few months in the military with a 19 year old.

Now I didn't need to spend as many hours at the Denny's. I did remain the return driver, however, and I did return to the Denny's for some pie a la mode, and to see the waitress again, who was now only one year older than me. She introduced some of her girlfriends who attended the University of Washington to my buddies. We went out on a date a few times. My buddies were enjoying the last months of their service. I was fortunate to spend Christmas of 1964 with her family. I was the first young man they knew who would go to Vietnam. I think of her and her family every Christmas.

My twentieth birthday didn't fall on Father's Day and I was still unable to be with my Dad. I was in Vietnam.

I don't know if I was responsible or mature then, but I do know that over the next several years there were many older Americans on the draft board who were supposed to be responsible and mature, and who sent thousands of young men to South East Asia.

The next time I visited my parents I was on my way from Vietnam to my next assignment. I stopped in Los Angeles for a few days on my way to Ft. Bliss, Texas. Ft. Bliss neighbors El Paso and is across the Rio Grande from Juarez, Mexico.

There was no wall. America was great.

When I arrived at Ft. Bliss there were few Vietnam veterans and it seemed as if everyone was preparing to leave for Vietnam. There wasn't much for me to do. So I spent many afternoons and nights across the river in Juarez.

It was an unusual transition from Vietnam to the "Real World." In Juarez there was no war, no demonstrations. If Vietnam came up in conversation, a blank expression would appear on a smiling Mexican face and they would say, "Why?" A blank expression would be on my face, unable to answer. I was sometimes thankful I didn't speak Spanish. In Juarez, you didn't need to be 18 or 21, mature or responsible to drink and have a good time. In many ways, it reminded me of Vietnam. It was a good place to temporarily forget about the war.

On a warm Wednesday night in June, I didn't go to Juarez. I went to a small quiet nightclub in El Paso, ordered a scotch and soda (again inspired from another song). I pulled out my California driver's license. It was the second time I turned twenty-one. It was my 21st birthday.

That new I.D. Card that replaced the one that was never lost? It was cut up and last seen floating down the Rio Grande. Now, that was being responsible.

After that, my need to cross the bridge to Mexico diminished, although I did make a few trips with some young troops headed to Vietnam. I felt responsible for them. I was beginning to grow up.

June nineteen, sixty-seven—I was out of the Army. Five years had passed since I had been with my Dad on Father's Day. We celebrated my 22nd birthday by going to the Los Angeles Dodgers' baseball game. I was feeling mature.

The memories of all the soldiers I served with are constantly with me, especially the older guys at Ft. Lewis, Washington. I thank them for feeling that at the age of 19, I was mature enough to be 21.

17

My Return Home From Vietnam

Wes Cloys

Tan Son Nhut Airport Saigon, Vietnam –
Saturday morning May 14, 1966

I was entering my last hours of my year-long overseas assignment. I had arrived in Saigon the night before. That Saturday morning we woke up early, ate breakfast and waited for the chartered commercial airliner that would return us to the "Real World." Before boarding the flight we were told that the plane would be on the airfield a very short time and that: "If your ass isn't on the plane when the pilot gets the okay to take off, you'll be left behind."

When the portable stairs rolled up to the airplane doors men were already running across the tarmac. Everyone was excited. I remember very little of that long flight home, except that the soldier seated next to me was from an Eastern State, New England or somewhere. His name, like mine, was Wesley. Around 7:PM sundown, Saturday, May the Fourteenth, the plane landed at Travis Airfield in California. Many of the guys coming down the stairs of the plane were laughing, yelling and falling down, and kissing the ground.

It was good to be home.

As we went through customs, our bags were checked and we had to answer questions. There was no welcome home and no thank you. Already I had a sense that we were in a different time. A group of us exited the airport and looked around. What do we do? We were on our own. There was no rifle over my shoulder. It felt odd because there were very few times in the past eleven months that I hadn't carried my M-14 with me. From the time I departed the troop ship, climbed down the stairs hanging on the side of the ship onto the landing craft, and then walked through the surf of Vietnam, my rifle was with me day and night. I had turned my rifle over to the Sergeant of Arms on the Friday before leaving for Saigon and the flight back. Now it was Saturday night, and I was in the United States.

Five to seven of us jumped into a taxi headed for the San Francisco airport. What a ride; freeways, bright lights, toll roads and cars that we had not seen for a year. We arrived at San Francisco airport and then I headed to Los Angeles. There was a flight every hour to Los Angeles and my flight was at 12:AM, arriving in L.A. at 1:AM. Some of the guys had a much longer wait. It was approximately 11:PM, and after buying my ticket, I made a collect phone call home. I called my parents (it was the first time in 371 days since I had heard their voices). They would pick me up at about 1:15AM, Sunday. While waiting for the flight a small group of us sat at a bar. We ordered real milk and hamburgers. No one spoke to us or offered us a drink. We noticed the clothing styles had changed. It was just the beginning of a changing world.

My parents picked me up at LAX. It was early Sunday morning. On to the Los Angeles freeways and heading home. I walked into the house. The kitchen had been remodeled. My bedroom was the same. We went to bed. On Sunday morning at 10:30, my dad woke me up and took me to church. At my church I was the first young soldier to come home from Vietnam. There would be many more young men to return, and two who never would.

I remember the hugging and the handshakes....

....after we drive home and I'm sitting on my parents' front porch, I feel alone. I'm thinking of my many friends who I've spent the past year with. Guys who I would never see or speak with again and I'm less than 48 hours from being in-country.

Connections
Life in the Military and Subsequent Effects on My Life

Roger E. Thurnell

It was the fountain that reminded me. Outside the Central Library in Downtown Los Angeles, they have a fantastic array of several geysers, waterspouts and waterfalls, some going up in the air, two dozen filling the pool that creates the waterfall effect. It gives one's eyes a choice of several resting places and allows one's ears to take in the soothing sounds of water falling from one pool to the next. However, the effect on the timbre of the sounds is different depending on where you are sitting or standing. Sometimes it sounds like a gentle spring and yet, just a few yards away, there is a violent crashing of agitated waters.

It's funny how the distinctive character, quality or tone of something can tap into our consciousness and bring back personal memories. Just the other day the fountains replicated the battering gush of rain assaulting the tin roofs of our barracks during the monsoon season in Thailand. The cacophony of sound reached your gut when violent winds drove the rain sideways and pummeled a hard barrage against your relatively flimsy cover they called a barracks. The very definition of a barracks is "a hut for temporary shelter." Oh boy....

That took me back to 1971 in the Air Force and the time when thoughts wandered, beliefs were challenged and there was a constant onslaught of new and different things that must be learned. It rained. And it rained. The unyielding showers had the cleansing ability to scour my young mind and soul so that I might take on new perspectives of what everyone was talking about. Often, they talked about Vietnam. At last, without the presence of my family or old friends to guide my thoughts in specific, already mapped-out ways, I was beginning, at last, to think for myself. I began to form my own opinions separately from others.

I had always been shy and held back from the rest of the world. But I had been lucky.

Just a few weeks before, when stationed at Kingsley Field,

Oregon, my buddy in the missile shop, Ed Bott, had told me so many great things about Thailand that I was encouraged to volunteer. And now, having wanted and hoped for this posting in Thailand, it was an unforeseen surprise that I had been given my orders so quickly. Just marvelous.

Upon arrival at Udorn Thani, I found myself in a beautiful country with fascinating people. I got busy learning as much as I could about the people and the place, and experiencing things that others didn't take the time to bother with. That was okay by me. Nearly all of the Thai people I met were good people and easy to like.

The unexpected contrast to me—I was just thrilled to be there—was hearing so many other guys in my barracks (and throughout our Air Force Base) wishing they were home and just counting the days to "get back to the world" (the United States). They couldn't stand being overseas.

I kept my opinions to myself, but I thought: *You dumb fools. You're just missing out. You're letting your previously socially inbred belief systems get in your way. I'm not gonna let that happen to me!* I cleared out every chance I got.

We started taking day trips out to the country, and immediately I found that being in Thailand turned out to be an experiential gold mine.

There were five of us G. I. buddies who invited the same number of Thai gals out on our little escapades. We went to Nong Khai, which was on a high bank where we could look across the Mekong River and see Vientiane, Laos. We went to Gumpa Wapi, the monkey village that not only had the little begging creatures hoping for a banana, but was also home to so many Thai Buddhist temples with astounding architecture amid the easygoing lives of wonderful Thai people. On other days there was Khan Khen and even a slow trip down the rails two hundred and fifty miles to Bangkok.

We went to Nong Walampoo, took a canoe out on the local river and were shown some distinctive sights and locations. Coming back to the village we ate at a local restaurant. One of the girls with us told me who was sitting at the next table. I turned to look and a friendly man smiled at me, and as we both stood and clasped hands he introduced himself as the Mayor of the town.

As opposed to other, discourteous G. I.'s, he recognized that the five of us along with our five Thai girls were okay, and we were welcomed. He then wrote, in beautiful Thai script, his name and instructions to anyone reading his note that I was welcome to call on him anytime I chose to. He was a very friendly and sincere man.

Of course all of those wonderful excursions had been in my off-times, the time away from my real job. My Air Force job. I was a Missile Guidance and Control Specialist. Most of the time I worked in the Missile Shop. It was a big, secluded revetment just off base. A revetment is a barricaded shelter or retaining wall that protects materiel. In this case, it was a fenced in, open area in which several steel and concrete dugouts contained our missiles that were adjacent to our missile shop.

From our barracks we got in our stretch pick-up and drove out there to begin our twelve-hour shift. We worked twelve on/twelve off for four days and then we'd get a couple of days off. (This was one of the factors that unknowingly prepared me for unique jobs as a delivery driver—including handling Air Freight Specials near LAX—in my future civilian life).

When we arrived, we started up the missile-testing console and then went out just forty yards to one of the revetments where the AIM-7's and AIM-9's were stored (the missiles that we referred to as "birds") to select the next one that needed to be tested. It took twenty minutes for the console to warm up, so grabbing the next bird, bringing it back to the shop, opening the canister and loading the missile onto the console worked out pretty good, timing-wise.

A clean bird might take only a half hour or so from beginning to end. One that needed more attention—removing and replacing a circuit board, or several circuit boards, replacing a warhead or finding one that had not been stored properly and was showing the effects of condensation and the subsequent rusting, would require more time. That meant we had to service the missiles and their containers as well. There were plenty of things to keep us busy, but all in all, it was a pretty good job we had in the rare luxury of an air-conditioned shop.

Each day we did pretty much the same kind of work. But one day, it suddenly changed. So I'll just tell you about that unexpected time, and one of those days, and the beginning of my modified consciousness.

It was a typical day in Thailand. At that time of year the days were long and hot, yet as I began testing air-to-air Sidewinders in our 70° Missile Shop I knew we had it made compared to many other workshops on base. It was 1971 and two hundred miles away the war in Vietnam was raging. Unexpectedly the Chief Master Sergeant said to me: "Sergeant, you and Tanaka take two other guys down to the Bomb Dump. They need help." My first thought was: *Damn, they must be bombing the shit out of 'Nam to have to help the bomb crews. That's a lot of killing.*

Our troops in Vietnam who fought the NVA and the Viet Cong had to think of killing, or they'd get their heads shot off or a bayonet in their guts. We weren't on the front lines, risking our lives. They were.

We got to the Bomb Dump and three dozen guys, shirts off and sweatin' like hell, were handling 500 pounders. There were crews of four; I looked for my buddy Juan Rael. Instead I saw Carlos who said: "Hey man, what's up?" I said: "I just brought some intelligent guys to help some 'dimwits' do their job, you know?" He smiled that sneaky grin of his and said: "Go and join Juan's team and I'll take your guys to form a new crew." Juan came over and said: "Hey Rick. C'mon over and give us a hand."

Compared to the complexity of the work we dealt with on our missiles, it was easy. Of course, we worked on hot asphalt in the sun with no shade or wind, and that heat was intense. That experience, and others like it, unknowingly paved the way for me to be able to perform the work required years later as a driver, during the long days in the hot months of the California desert. But right now, it seemed unbearable.

Bombs were delivered by cranes and dozens of them placed onto racks. We inserted fuses into the warheads and the final arming was done on the flight line before loading. I gotta say, those bomb crews were good. They knew their business and worked hard at a mind-numbing pace, one lot after another.

We kept at it for about three hours and then went over and hugged the wall of the nearest building with some shade and took a break. With legs on the ground and backs to the wall, we sat dazed in our sweat and stench and let our minds wander.... I looked back at the revetment with crews hustling and saw evenly spaced rows of metallic monsters with fins. Dark grey-green fish without souls, yet within them a dormant heart of unlit fire waiting only for a spark that would ignite death around them.

I was pulled two different ways.

I felt I had accomplished something and yet, as time passed, my thoughts shifted as a rising sense of guilt questioned what I was really doing. I knew the missiles we worked on—the AIM-7's and AIM-9's—allowed our pilots protection in the skies and gave them the ability to bring down their Soviet-made MiG's. And yet haunting images crept into my mind of bodies being mutilated by the bombs we delivered. We had worked like hell to arm those things and yet I wondered how many innocent women and children would perish from stray bombs in our attempt to win this war. It was weeks later that I found that a lot of guys wondered about that and felt the same as me. That was one of the reasons that, by the time I got back to the states, I applied as a Conscientious Objector.

But not everyone felt that way. There is no question that the Vietnam War was controversial. Differences in the strategies and tactics of the top brass and the hawkish suggestions by our congressional leaders were often at cross-purposes. We wanted to fight that war and win. Or we wanted to negotiate. Or do it this way or that way or.... Politics intervened, and other factors prevented us from reaching conclusions while our troops were dying by the thousands. What bothered me was the all too abundant presence of ignorance laden with hate displayed by so many guys over there.

Quite a few just wanted to kill as many "gooks" as possible. Hmmph. I had been in-country for seven months, met dozens of Vietnamese refugees who had crossed the Laotian highlands and into Thailand to escape the war and they were not a threat. Those fools who reduced our efforts to a racial issue just displayed their built-in prejudice fed by ignorance. They found their bias in the different facial features of the Asian peoples. They didn't realize the significance of the epicanthic fold above their eyes that made the coarsest of our G.I.'s refer to them as "slant-eyes." The truth was that, having dealt with the merciless windstorms carrying dust throughout the summer months, and the blinding snowstorms of winter for tens of thousands of years, mutations that were necessary in that part of the world transformed the Asians' bodily structures over time. It protected their eyes and honed their bodies down to the short, squat shapes often associated with the Eskimos. Those foolish G.I.'s only found another reason to hate. They couldn't stand change or differences.

Even General Westmoreland said: "The Oriental doesn't put

the same high price on life as the Westerner. Life is cheap for the Oriental."

Personally, I'm glad I grew up liking the variety I found in people. I like the diversity in varying body types. I like the fact that there are people on our planet that have a broad range in the color of their skin. Today, I feel honored to have come across people from well over a hundred and fifty different nations of our world: all of them different, all of them unique.

Just then another bomb dump team came our way to catch a breather. We went back and worked bombs by the hundreds for three hours, took a break and then worked another three hours. Totally wiped out when we finished, we crowded into step-vans to head back to the barracks, glad that shit was over. We'd meet up later at Juan's place. I got cleaned up, changed and headed uptown.

There were maybe twenty people at Juan's bungalow. Carlos, a Puerto Rican from the Bronx, had a unique kind of craziness you admired. Bernard Crumpton (who we called Crump), from the South Side in Chicago, was a quiet guy with a brilliant mind. Juan, from Albuquerque, had this infectious laugh that was utterly contagious and always got us in a good mood. I can still hear the echoes of his laugh today. His girlfriend Yuli, her back hunched by the scoliosis of her spine since birth, was surprisingly elegant in her actions. Dark smiling eyes revealed the secrets of her unassuming beauty. There was another guy there. I never knew his name, but I looked up to him for the way he carried himself. After Vietnam he came over to Thailand and was a real stand-up guy. And that's what I called him—"Stand-up."

That night some guys smoked weed and others snorted red rock heroin. We all had our own way to blow off steam and yet we looked out for each other. I was swiggin' down a bottle of Singha beer that some—including me—called formaldehyde, but I didn't care. I liked it. It went down easy. And, I had some Mekong whiskey to sip, to trim the edge off my disgust at those images I had earlier at the bomb dump....

I was watching Stand-up and Carlos across the room and then I noticed some smartass who claimed to be a friend of Juan's take something out of his pocket and hold it in his hand.

Curious, I saw him flip the cover of his Ronson, light it up and when that thing in his hand flared up, Juan yelled: "Hey, what the hell are you—" The guy threw it on the ground. It was a fuckin' cherry bomb and it sounded like a bomb had dropped!

Stand-up hit the deck flat-out with hands over his head as if to protect himself from shrapnel. Juan shouted: "What the fuck ya doin? He's just back from the *'Nam*, ya goddamn fool!'" Crump and I grabbed that guy and hustled him out the door and saw him bounce his way down the steps to the bottom of the stairs. Nobody gave a shit if he broke a leg or landed on his head. We never saw that sorry son-of-a-bitch again.

I turned back and saw Carlos on his knees. He had also spent a year in 'Nam. He and Stand-up were okay, but shaken. My imagination told me that in that ragged moment of time, their lives had been suspended like the dew on a spider's web—and now those drops had been spread out on the floor like tears falling in the aftermath of war.

Scared half to death, Yuli melted into Juan's arms, her tears opening a flood of action. Crump and I helped Carlos and Stand-up to rise from the floor. Carlos took a deep breath, glanced around and said, "Hey. It's over. We're okay." Crump and I went around the room to make sure everyone was okay. It took a while, but we all settled down and found ourselves grateful to be amongst friends.

Many times over the years since then I used to think of days like that and it really put me into a funk 'cause I really missed those guys. I missed the special bond we had. And I missed the great experiences I had with so many other friends I had known in different locales—all of the unique places I had been stationed. But the years had passed … and finally, I remembered some of the bad shit, too.

Following Thailand, I was stationed at Grand Forks Air Force Base in North Dakota. For two years I lived in the barracks on base, along with a bunch of mischievous and rowdy guys that were exploring the possibilities of getting high on one drug or another. It was just as well. Going from a hundred degree jungle atmosphere to the "NoDak" winter blizzards—one time pegging the needle at ninety degrees below zero—was a two hundred degree shift in temperature we had to be acclimated to. Luckily, a friend of mine, still stationed in Thailand, was sending me holiday greetings cards from time to time. Oh boy! The best cards I've ever received!

I will not explain the process (though I know it well) how he took the finest Thai weed, cut and sifted it, put it in a baggie and sealed it and found a way to crush the contents down to a sliver of width that could be inserted into the greeting card and sent to me. He sent me three of these cards over the first few months that I was in North Dakota, easily and successfully getting past the sniffer-dogs that were so prevalent in those times.

I turned on quite a few guys with a couple of tokes of my "special ciggies." Many of the guys at Grand Forks I had known at Kingsley Field in Oregon before departing for Thailand. I had been known and respected then, but now these little bits of inhaled sunshine in the middle of a minus forty-degree winter made me a bit popular. That was a good thing for a while, but other unresolved issues were yet to come to fruition and disrupt my mental state of being. In my last year of service I went through a period of time that proved to be unsettling, and put a whole new perspective on my beliefs.

I suppose it began by hearing such things as "baby-killers," or guys being spit on when they arrived back home from Vietnam. When I voluntarily joined the Air Force, I was the epitome of John Wayne in a gung-ho attitude. My Dad had been in World War II and had been an important player in contributing to the plan to bring to justice certain Nazi leaders after we had won the war. In the months following Victory in Europe, he had interrogated the wives of top leaders of the Reich, including Rudolf Hess (Hitler's right-hand man for two decades until he had parachuted into England) and Sepp Dietrich, who was one of Hitler's most influential warriors who had helped to create the Waffen SS (the tank division composed only of the highly feared SS troops). My father remained in Germany right up to the beginning of the Nuremberg War Trials.

Here I was in "the armpit of the world" … in other words, in North Dakota. I was wondering what the hell I was doing in this ridiculous war that had come to a virtual stalemate in 1973. In that last year, as the frigid winds were howling outside the barracks and we were all confined to a sedentary existence, memories kept creeping back over and over again.

The greatest fear guys had at that time was of the Military Police invading the barracks and busting guys for the drugs we were so engaged in. Yet that never bothered me. I never worried about being busted.

My thoughts were elsewhere. I was just afraid to confront people. I was scared to death to be seen—to be associated with the killings in Vietnam. I would step out of my room and be thwarted by a long empty hallway, seemingly sterile yet filled with the images of those bodies, thanks to my missiles and my bombs. Did we kill them? Or did we murder them? My self-confidence was shot to hell and I felt that my heart and soul had been tampered with—trampled by the lies and half-truths thrown at me for the past three years due to a controversial war. That frame of mind—that depression—was continually present and lasted four or five months.

I reached up to wipe the sweat from my forehead and took a deep breath. Opening my eyes, I saw the water falling peacefully from one fountain to another. I let out a big sigh....

....and shake my head to clear it and stand up. I begin again to hear the music of the waterfalls outside the library. Jesus. It sure is good to be back. I have never been more proud for having applied as a Conscientious Objector during that War.

I look around and remember that today I'm surrounded by men and women, civilians and Veterans—all of whom have unexpected abilities to relieve my haunted thoughts and to heal the wounds of war *and* each other in whatever way we can.

And I am glad.

"Do you know my first name?"

Denise M. Woodard

The phone rings in my office, and the sergeant answers. "Morning, sir. ... Uh yes, I'll check, hold please."

The sergeant says to me, "Lieutenant, it's Colonel Danford."

I pick it up and say, "Good morning, sir."

Colonel Danford wasn't in our unit, but he'd worked with me briefly on a small project we coordinated for him in our small military community in Europe.

"Hey there Denise," he drawled as if we'd been friends for some time. "You know I've been in the Army a long time, and I'd like to talk with you about your career. I think I can help."

Colonel Danford was in the same Army officer branch I was and there was a tradition of officer mentorship in the Army, so I accepted his offer of a conversation. It felt as if the clouds were beginning to part, and there might be a little sun.

You see I had filed a complaint under the new sexual harassment guidelines. A complaint about hostile, sexually charged jokes directed at me in the field by my commander, another commander, and one of the senior NCOs working for them. It didn't matter that I was the officer who had planned, organized and coordinated the entire field exercise.

I was the only female officer in the field, and once we were out there I was the target of hostility. But the hostile jokes were just part of the picture. I was also dismissed and ignored as a participant in the exercise.

The problems at the field exercise were a last straw. The jokes and the tone were bad, but they were nothing compared to the dangerous results of the misogyny that existed in our unit, and I learned later, at the level of command above us, my boss's boss.

The wife of one of our soldiers had been hospitalized more than once after severe beatings from her husband, PFC Maldonado. Eileen had been a soldier in our unit too, and had married PFC Maldonado a few months after he arrived in-country and in-processed to our company. She decided not to re-enlist after she had their baby, and she stayed in-country in family quarters with her husband.

One day our medical officer, a doctor, called me when my company commander was out of town. His frustration was palpable; I felt like I could hear his pulse pounding through the phone. Eileen was in the hospital again, bruised over her whole body, and the Medical Officer said that if someone doesn't stop her husband, "He's going to kill her!" That was the first I had heard of the multiple severe beatings and hospitalizations for Eileen. The commander had kept that information on the down low.

The commander never separated the couple. He could have ordered the husband to live in the barracks, and ordered him to stay away from his wife and child. He could have arranged supervised child visits. He could have investigated the husband for assault under the Uniform Code of Military Justice, but he didn't do any of those things.

What this French Fry of a Commander did in response to the beatings was to try and order an annulment for PFC Maldonado, without his knowledge. The couple was Catholic, and so was I. And I say the annulment was for PFC Maldonado because in the commander's mind it was to help him, not Eileen. One day he walked into my office and said, "I want you to go to the Catholic Chaplain and apply for an annulment for PFC Maldonado." My surprise and lack of words must have seemed like a question to him, for he continued as if to answer: "There's absolutely nothing wrong with Maldonado that won't be solved when he gets rid her. She eggs him on. She gets what she's asking for!"

I explained to the commander that annulments don't work that way. The Catholic Church won't grant an annulment based on a request from a commander.

Months later I saw Eileen and her child in town. She had gotten a divorce and they were moving back to the states. She had a lot to say, and I listened. She told me she had asked the commander over and over for help, but he had done nothing.

As for my sexual harassment complaint, it was my word against the commander's word, and we were the only two officers in our unit. The complaint was noted, and no action was taken. I still worked for the French Fry, and he hated me. A few months later I received a retaliatory Officer Evaluation Report, a report so negative that it would almost certainly prohibit my promotion to captain and ensure that I would have to leave the Army at the end of my term after failing to be promoted.

I knew the report was false, but getting proof and witnesses was an uphill battle. Nevertheless, I began the process of appealing the Officer Evaluation Report. I needed any support I could get, and I asked Colonel Danford if he could testify about my work performance on the project we had coordinated for him. I showed him the negative OER, and he wrote a complimentary letter about the small amount of work I did with him.

It was a week or so later that he called my office that morning offering to talk with me about my career. Grateful for the hope, and for a chance to talk with someone outside my command chain, I thanked him, and he quickly closed the conversation saying, "Great. We'll do it on Friday after work. I know a little place away from here, and it will be easier to talk there. I'll meet you at the community club, and we'll go from there." Click.

In my early twenties, I was one who would almost feel guilty for not taking someone at the face value of his word, but I quickly went to the Wise Sage of our unit, the civilian secretary Joan, wife of an Army colonel everyone respected. What did Joan think about meeting after work for a conversation? "Officers do this all the time," she said. And it was true. Officers met for drinks and discussed work all the time.

On the Friday of our meeting I went home, changed out of my uniform into some pants and a shirt, and as an afterthought put on a coat long enough to cover my shapeliness. Colonel Danford, probably thirty years older than I, wore his shirt unbuttoned about a third of the way down, and had gold chains decorating his gray chest hair. As soon as I got in his car his gestures had all the vibes of a date. Putting his arm around me to open and close the car door, almost putting his arm around me as he opened the door into the quiet little restaurant. It almost would have been polite if the situation had been a date, but it felt manipulative because he hadn't asked me on a date. He had offered to have a conversation with me about my career.

We sat at a table, and I talked openly about the status of my appeal, and how frustrating it was to have to continue working under the same commander after I had filed a sexual harassment complaint against him. Still hoping he meant to advise me, I nursed one beer while he had more. His response to all I had said was,

"Denise, you don't even know my first name, do you?" With three quarters of one strong beer in me, I hesitated, then envisioned his signature block and said, "Michael" as if it was a crossword puzzle I was trying to solve. He laughed. How stupid I suddenly felt. I was embarrassed I hadn't known all along that he was after something other than helping me.

Next he informed me that he and his wife Laura, a blond woman like me but maybe a decade older, with a substantial management position in a civilian office, were getting a divorce. He said he could tell I was something of a conservative girl by the way I still had my coat on, so he wouldn't ask me to do anything until he was divorced, but then when he was divorced, we could go ahead. The way he said it, the tone, the way one eyebrow lifted and his head turned oozed sex, but he never said the words. People usually don't.

I cringed at my stupidity. I felt like I had a rock in my stomach because Colonel Danford's call had given me hope of being heard and of being taken seriously. I said, "I think I'd like to go home now sir." I was quiet on the way back, and as we approached the post, he said, "Hey Denise, I haven't seen your legs yet. Next time wear a skirt, okay, baby?" I was as silent as a stone as he drove me to my Bachelor Officer Quarters. I'd left the lamp by my window on so I could see when I opened the front door. As he pulled up to let me out, he asked if that lamp was in my bedroom. I shut the car door pretending I didn't hear what he had said.

The next time Colonel Danford called my office I told him any further conversations between us would need to be at the workplace during work hours. I had some documents to deliver to his office, and when I took them over we were both professional. As I walked out the door he said, "Say Denise," and I turned around, "Yes, sir?" He put both hands straight up in the air as if we were in a western film and I had just burst through the saloon doors with a pistol pointed straight toward him. He said, "Remember, I never offered you anything other than help on your appeal." "Yes, sir. I understand." And I did understand that if I suggested to anyone that he had proposed a sexual relationship he wouldn't hesitate to call me a liar.

I won my appeal by asking for an independent investigation. The Investigator interviewed unit members and reported that documents my commander had accused me of losing were found in his own desk drawer along with a letter, dated months earlier, from DoD telling me I was due to be considered for promotion and outlining the procedures for submitting my application. If an officer fails to prepare and submit her own promotion packet correctly and on time the officer will be passed over for promotion, and will have a slim chance of staying in the Army.

It was the commander's responsibility to give me that letter, but he had deliberately kept it from me.

I left active duty to go to graduate school, which was my plan all along, and I was promoted to captain when I took a position in the Army National Guard during Operation Desert Storm.

This is a true story, but the names have been changed for the privacy of the people involved.

5 minutes

Eric Fleming

The bright valley sun has sunk in me. My black ops clothes
sweat with the cling,
heavy the heat my window seat. The dragon's teeth.
The adjustments
I have to make the wave, the energy, the chi …
the beauty to surface of today.

Clean Faces

Eric Fleming

I see the slick commercials,
the jobs on high — they — the Apaches fly on by.
No blood, mud or battles yet.
Yeah want some?
Get some.
Join some be some,
Be all you can be, son.
Yeah I do, we do.
Do you?
The war's an image without the taste,
The feeling
The grit the spit,
the whole one two with the jingle jangle of a mess kit.
Let's wrap it up place it above on high.
Fresh faces so nice so clean the tough look,
the mean the one-time battle dream forms
patriotic painted faces.
Get some get some, if ya want some.

Dream House

Eric Fleming

Dream house way
Long house way
I haven't told gram-mi something in a-long while
The source mind
huh that's a good way of dreaming in the real world
Walking
stepping kicking out everyday life
Spilling into caterpillar's cocoon for compassion of comparison
I like that
mother earth masters of the universe
Self All because she guessed
The dreaming of the ancient one
Oh gammy
good job
I love you
See you next time by the dream horse rocking chair
Bless our futures
catching the wave
the change
I will be waving
I will see you there

To Be or Not

Eric Fleming

To be a Warlord

You should at least shoot your friend in the back of the head

Get a feel for wonder of war

The agenda

The greatness of it

Spread so thick-wild wheels spinning in my head

Where to meet the models at?

At this party

At this club

A mess of war profits

A sand of success

A war is long short

Home before Christmas

It's still a bitch

A heavy burden

Who wants some

Enough for a party for

all

How low can you go?

Eric Fleming

I step across the desert in softly sinking sand, shifting beneath me, with black leather stripped toed jungle boots, catching, kicking sandy crystals out towards our burn pit. Time is pushing me, and Stan. The mission is to get going. Dark purple violet clouds—the night is hanging close at hand. SSG Dun sun wants his pit burnt. So yeah, I'll set it ablaze. We're going to be motoring out of here, gone for a day or two. Can't wait to getting it on, on this dark sandy road. Chill-in the shiny-lit sky, burn bright tonight. Blackout light business in the front, fire party to the back. Fuck yeah and yahoo. I tell Stan I got this—to get going and to finish his checks on his vehicle. Our two-man convoy is waiting, almost ready to go. One last thing to do, then off and away from the main unit.

SSG Dun sun—the machine gun tilting—tightening his belt, aiming at me—always at me—trying to ruin a parade, in a managed, worried way. Dealing with me, what he thinks. I might too, as squared away as I can be, a loose cannon too. Soon as he steps around, he says, "Did ya do this? Check that?"

I think, Yeah, motherfucker it's done. Like I always do.

It's going to be fun tonight on the long road ahead with my peace and quiet on my time, on target. We are close to the front line. There is a medical unit that is farther back and they have an extra water buffalo we are going to pick up for our company, and yeah hot showers maybe, and the even better chow than we already have. Life usually is better as you get closer to the rear. And women—because we don't got none. Not in this unit, Charlie Co 54th Combat Engineers.

I am going off for a while stepping to another grid, yep happy step-pin inside. I am in the top lower lip of Charlie Co's burn pit; I am looking down at strewn around-thrown down-garbage-paper trash that flows to hard crusty packed sand. Standing, looking, surveying the mo gas soaked land. All I have to do is light it and walk away. A piece of paper, something to start a fire. I look at the trash-jumbled heap, the ground. Aahhh ... I find it and grab a nice full size sheet of used white copy paper. I twist it, tear it, and turn its shape so I will get a good even burn. I take my lighter to the torn piece of paper ... and boom! I think I hear someone scream for his mom. I don't know for sure but my gut is telling me this is an emergency to hear the note my brain has just sent me just move faster please. A lot is going on, I hang on long enough to process, spit and chew. I have my eyes closed off and I am inside. A quiet calm voice says: You really fucked up this time, Fleming. I'll check on this. I need to confirm this because I don't feel anything. No pain No emotions of terror. Always a weird feeling of calm, of two entities locked in this dark space within my mind together. Forgetting time is moving on with or with out me. Sense of touch smell shut down. My eyes pop open then snap shut my sight the only window to my mind my intuition of my animal kicks in cause I see fire, the reds oranges and yellows. I snap back into reality. There is a fire.

I got one shot to figure this out. I either walk into the fire or I walk out.

Flipping to quick action emergency spinning my body turning to the left side moving shifting sliding spinning to my right using my back as a shield for my front. This much I can do. Flames on my face catch the top of my head my hair my rifle and equipment along for the ride. I can't see can't shake this fire but I figure I am on the ramp maybe heading towards the top. I jump and leap as far as I can. A good dive stretched out like a scared Superman I land crawling scraping slamming my face and head against the hard packed sand a head-butting experienced madman, smacking whacking his head face neck, along the way up I jump again, stop drop and roll. I do quick hops and throw my body out farther from the pit, dive from my knees to get out. My mind flashes to a vision and gives me a feeling, as if walking casually thinking of deep white sandy snow showering me. I go with it. I try deep diving, to go under the Iraqi desert. I then think I am in a pool, and crash my forehead into the concrete-side, using it as a guide scraping against it, using my face as a plow to get to the bottom. Try to feel for any depth, any hope. This stop drop and roll shit is not working here. Fuck, that's all I really got. I slam my face my body, jumping out towards the ground because I know the fire is still with me, on me, trying to melt me on the top of this earth. I need a deeper river. I jump out on hope for the deep sand, my last desperate dive my right and left hand outstretched going for all. I feel softer shallow sand.

Face first. I keep jumping into it. This is my chance. Fuck not deep enough. I am rolling like a fool, throwing sand in my face, rubbing it in, scratching it in as fast as I can. Can anyone see me? Help me? I am alone until a shadow moving in the light, gliding, chasing me finally envelops me in darkness. It shakes me. I am rolled over. Someone checks me, pats me. I open my eyes. See a winter parka. Madurski is smothering me.

"Eric, dude, you alright? Holy shit, man, me and the Lt were standing right over there."

I am spring-loaded, up on my feet. I hear the surprise in his voice of what just happened and how I came out of that fireball and smoky black pit. Other people come running from Charlie Co that is camped over on the other side of the compound. I look there, trying to orientate myself and to figure out what has just happened. My adrenaline is flowing. I am mad agitated. I feel like a cornered dog as everyone tries to corral me, tries to sit me down. I pace and switch directions, half bent, walking and weaving thru the mobile kitchen trailer heaters recently filled with fresh water. I am dodging people, not looking at them. I recognize them only by their voices. I am a little worried. It feels as if a candle is dripping down my face. I feel the warm liquid slowing to a trickle just above the lip of my sweet cleft. I think, Where's my weapon? I say out loud, "Where's my weapon?" If my weapon got burnt up too, it would just be sad, adding insult to injury. Multiple people say, "It's on your back, Fleming!"

Oh yeah, I have it strapped to my back. I check with my right hand, stretching toward my back, I feel the round barrel of my rifle. They have something for me to sit on. They ask me to sit down. As I do the front site post of my rifle immediately jams me up. I'm stuck on the lip of the rim tipping the 5-gallon oilcan every time I try to seat myself. I'm jammed up, hung up on the balancing act—at the same time the bottom of the rifle's pistol grip, rubbing, wedging its turned hard edge between my ribs. I'm doing mini-squat thrusts of pain. I don't want to continue to add to the soup/sandwich of this fiery barbecue. I focus on the front metal sight post stuck on the tin can rim. I snatch at, grip it, wrapping palm, fingers to feel around to the barrel where the metal swivel and the black cloth shoulder strap meet. I grab and push the weapon violently, sliding it up and off my ribs, using the black sling as guide. Feeling the hand guard on my ribs, the weapon is horizontal front site post to butt, the weapon is level now. I am done with barbecue sandwiches and soup for the day.

My weapon comes off. My other equipment, too. I don't want to. It's mine. I am responsible. Once you give your weapon away, you're lost. It grounds me. It's always with me. I sit on the turned over 5-gal can. The bottom isn't painted camouflage, and I see shadowy gold shimmering light reflecting, peeking and leaking from under the fire lit night.

I tip and teeter with damaged new, nervous energy. I still feel the leaking. My mind focuses on this, trying to assess the damage. I don't know what to do. I'm sitting here now hunched over. Someone asks if I want water for my face. I look up; day is almost gone, fading into golden yellow-lit purple light, haze streaking, fading into a moon night. Yeah sounds good. Okay yes, I nod my head. Specialist Matthews gets water from the MKT 10-gal can for heating water. I thought we had a medic. They grab one of the silvered colored large ladles and pour it on the front part of my face and head. I feel it. I don't like it. I turn away to lessen the effect. I am sitting, now standing, talking to the medic. He is here on my left. Hey it's Frazier. Alright! He tells me I'm lucky because before we got him, he was working in the burn unit in Frankfurt. Yeah I like that. I feel a little better. There is a leak still going on. But I am done. I check out and go along for the ride. Lead follow or get the fuck out of the way. We are in a Humvee. Specialist Driben is driving. The medic, Doc Frazier, is asking questions. I'm in and out of reality—more gaps and holes are being punched in here for me. The questions, answers burn to forgotten memory. I am a follower of Frazier and he holds the gold I need for me.

I am quiet as we arrive to a unit with a lot of generators and air conditioning units, humming, pumping along. The sun is down now. A dark door opens on a trailer. We step up and into an office filled light. They sit me down and start checking, asking questions. One of the first questions is how's my breathing, my throat? Yeah my throat does hurt from inhaling smoke and fumes. I smell of the Mo gas. It's in the air, in my breath. I tell the doctor it's not too bad. I get the lights into the eyes, and all that, till I am laying on the white paper. I relax now and wait for any news on how bad I fucked up. I look at the ceiling and the greenish light paint mixing, interweaving with the lights. I stare at it. I realize I am cold. Why is it so cold in here? Oh yeah they got air conditioning. Oh that's right, that's what it feels like. It's nice and cool but I don't really like it right now. I think about a blanket. Be quiet. Better that way I think, so I stare at the ceiling until the Major comes back. He says something to the female medic about cleaning my face, and scrubbing it to get any and all debris out. Okay, I just look at him and follow his conversation. She goes to it. Best thing to do is be silent in the pain. I am embarrassed. My face is finally aired dry as I lay here waiting for the doctor to return. I have nice cold skin. I don't want to move.

The Major comes back. He tells me about a white paste of lotion with silver mixed in that's good for healing burns. He says we will see how my face/skin looks each day and how fast it heals, then he can say for sure how bad the damage. The medic wraps my whole head like a mummy around and around we go. You don't want any infections, the Major says. So you're going to be coming back twice a day to check, wash your face and re-due your bandages. Hey sir, can I get something for the pain later on? I know this shit is gonna be uncomfortable later when I try to fall asleep. We are living out of vehicles, and or tents, in the middle of the desert with cool to winter cold at night, and a nice hot steady blazing heat during the day. I don't know how my burnt face skin is going to react to this environment and how I am going to feel when all the shock and awe I put on me wears off. It's time to go. With my head dressed, face fucked and wrapped tight, I shake the bottle of pills the Major hooked me up.

I am the night breeze, nervous sweat, dripping from the inside, the visible man with observation thru eye-holes, head swiveling twisting turning practicing to get a feeling of depth as we step down thru the trailer light, the door swings open, my eyes try to adjust towards the Humvee parked in the darkness bathed in moonlight. I am riding gliding along, the smooth pills in my throat soon to be asleep in my head.

Man, those pills work great. That is what I think; face down on my green nylon cot, drippy drool from my mouth. My uniform, my boots still on. Fuck a blanket, my poncho liner or sleeping bag to keep me warm. I am right next to the HeadQuarters Track with a small tarp as cover. Fuck it I am ready to go, step into the day.

But wait, I look around as I sit on my cot. Alright, what am I supposed to do? My start time for the day, routine is halted, gone for now. The day and my company are full on. I have slept in.

Charlie Company and the Battalion carry on and continue with the clean up, demo missions of ammunition, explosives, rockets, weapons, Tanks, Bulldozers that the enemy has abandoned in open pits and/or hiding in some bunker complex. Destroy everything we can so the enemy doesn't roll back and use against us. Because soon will be going to a new AO. Fuck me I won't be going along. I'll be stuck right here bored out of my fucking mind. Fuck, this is the fun, serious tangible glue of a war sticking to a solider. I've been on maybe ten so far. I want more please. Fine time to blow yourself up. I need to hurry up this healing. We aren't going to be around here too much longer. It's winding down for us and, possibly soon after, I'm going back to the world if I don't reenlist. Maybe I'll go back to school, try out a community college for a while. I like going with my 1st platoon friends. Usually it's Corey, Grayson and The Lt when we're out in the wide open sky and sea of sand as you listen to your tunes or the music they have mic-ed up in the track, roaming, looking for anything worthy that's been left behind. Oakley's raging your face the first time you feel the shock wave of your own demo cooking off. Corey in the driver's seat, Lt as TC. Standing up in the back troop hatch, Grayson and I share an Ohh shit moment. As soon as we see the black smoke ball rolling up with sound right behind it, we duck down in cover of the M113 with puckered asshole surprised smiles. The holy shit faces lock up tight. Scared as shit. Together with a boom. A wave of energy coming at you. Thru you. Sitting, idling in the M113 supposedly at a safe distance. Corey guns it. Grayson and I hang on, looking at each other with the O face. Laughing with my friends.

I look at my black-strapped watch. Foggy in the head, G-shock says ten thirty hrs almost eleven hundred. I stand up and line up with the shade of the track vehicle. One side of this M113 is my bedroom wall. I stick to the shade of the day moving right next to Dewey's HQ track. Dewey comes around the corner of the HeadQuarters track. What's up Flem? Dewey says, a reddish hair soldier with a happy smile. Hey Fleming, Sgt said I'm supposed to look after ya, take care of ya. Driben will be driving ya back and forth.

Alright I say. I am squinting, staring away from the sun. My sunglasses; Oakley's gone in the fire. My little sister bought those sunglasses in December before I came back from emergency leave. Here I am missing my pink-framed Oakley's. I used a permanent black sharpie to take care of the color. Works pretty good. Just reapply the black marker once a month when the pink starts fading back thru. I miss my sunglasses. Feel bad for the loss of a nice gift and no backup for the sun. I am not hungry. Don't care about food. Have to keep moving forwards unfucking myself. That is what I got to do. I move towards Dewey. He unwraps my bandages. He wants to see my face, check it before I go see the Major again. He studies me in the late morning, still smiling, says good job Fleming. Says how his brother got burnt in a fire when he lived back in California. Vitamin E helped his brother's scarring and he had third degree burns. He applies my soft gel vitamin E tabs to my face. I am groggy waiting for the Medic. Dewey said he's also coming by to look at me too, before I go back to the doctor. Dewey leaves me, comes back with a folding stool. Sit down, he says. I'm going to build you a new house, hook you up, Flem dog. He takes the tarp used to cover the M113. A very large rubber-like tarp and attaches it to the side of the M113 track, like a super lean-to with sides. Dewey is laughing out loud as he works. I just sit there looking at him, squinting, trying to stay in the shade. I had enough heat for a while. Dewey's still laughing, a white boy straight out of Oakland. I think Los Angeles. It's in California? I wish I were there right now. How lucky do you have to be to live there? Dewey David Cole was always telling you that he was named after his father's best friend from Vietnam.

Fleming, I don't think I have ever seen Frazier move that fast before in my LIFE. He starts with the L then pauses and hits the I briefly, and then emphasizes the F and the E. He's still laughing. What? I don't know what he's talking about so I can't really enjoy what the fuck is going on. What? I say. Frazier, he says. Yeah? I say. Dewey, you know, Charlie Company's medic, yeah I say Dewey I've never seen him move so fast. He's so laid back usually. He ran across the compound, yelling someone's on fire. A short clip runs thru my head of a fiery explosion and our stocky medic running beating feet. I wonder what my dumb ass looked like. Running around the desert being chased by reds oranges and yellows bright light shining on me, beating my face, jumping, crawling in the sandy dark almost-lit moon night. I hear the Humvee. Driben is here. It's my ride back thru the day. Silence is usually a good friend. I can dive-in deep, settle for the ride. I wonder why no one from the company has asked me what happened. I am lost on that—clueless and curious. I take the ride back to the medical unit. Lucky for me it's camped a few miles from us. I sit in the back, silently looking at half overcast day. Clouds shifting, turning on and off sun light as they drift and we drive by. This is going to be the routine. Wake up, shuffle to the door, Humvee, medical steam-cleaned and checked twice a day. Riding back, popping pills. My cot stop drop plop and roll. It works well with silent cool darkness. With bandages and the heat the sweat the swirl, sandy dirt infection not good for me now. Doctor gave me profile of can do, nothing till his say.

I have nothing to do. But I got this beautiful no memory deep abandoning sleep. No memories of when I eat or piss. First night going into the first day feels like two days into three. That's what it feels like to me when SSG Dickhead from our S-3 wakes me up with this loud voice. I am a little freaked out. With wide eyes I look into his face. His facial expression stretches out before me like Dr. M.C. Coy from *Star Trek*. He is bugging me with his oblong head and hair receding high. His flashlight is reflecting with a slick yellow sticky sickening rusty red color against the green of the tarp as if my new home is wet inside and out. Why is it raining? I hear a generator. Specialist Fleming! We are going to send you back as soon as we can. Wagner's going back for his baby's delivery and we're going to put you on the next one out, send you back to Germany. I am swinging my head back and forth and around. Craning my neck to see what the fuck is going on. Batman loud with his light has crashed thru the dark night and into the track covered rubber skinned opening. Making contact of a four-sided doorway, swoosh with a whack every time he enters. What time is it? Are we moving out? I am swinging my head like a bandaged cat. His talking is louder and more concise. We have Chinooks coming in. You're not the top priority. But you're about third or fourth on the battalion list. I hear something about other people getting hurt, more babies. I think, What the fuck is this? What? What the fuck is going on? Back? Fuck! Everyone else is going to be here. I got one chance to finish this, ride the rest of it out with everyone else. Fuck you, I think. The doctor never said anything about going back to Germany. I hear myself interrupting SSG Dickhead, answering him with a surprised, No, Sergeant I'm not going back. He's shocked by my loud voice filling the space with one small word no. I see the look of why don't you want to go back? I tell him, The Major never said that. He's all confused. I interrupt him with a no every time. I'm whacked out, lying in my cot, drugged up, trying to have a little less conversation please! I got to go back to sleep. Back? Yeah I better watch my back. These motherfuckers are trying to get rid of me. Doing me a favor? Who am I going to hang out with? Oh, Shit! I forgot about the ether bunny. I got to keep an eye out for him, too. He could get me. The Staff Sergeant finally agrees with the condition that I get a note from the doctor tomorrow when I go see him. I want to stay here so that's what I'm going to do. Fuck this, I have to try to go back to sleep with this fucking rumor going around. There is this dentist assistant who happens to have access to ether and he's going around raping dudes. Just before we go to sleep, we fuck around, yelling, Don't let the ether bunny get ya! Truth or not—I don't want to find out now how it feels to be an ether bunny victim. Batman leaves my area of operation, snapping the flaps opened and closed, giving his last known irritating presence away.

I wake to Dewey. I can hear him say, You got mail. I look up checking the mail carrier's hair color, still wary. Status is? I go back to sleep cause I saw Dewey's reddish hair but mindful to be on the lookout. I sleep till it's time to go back. Get that note. Get more pills. Basically the same routine. Driven back and forth a couple more days. Feels like a week. Someone asks about how the female medics look. The mail piles up on my cot. The *Rolling Stone*, muscle magazines, the plastic protectors spill its slippery sliding mail wave, spreading thick. Mail in a war zone has its ebbs and flows and it's finally catching up with us now. A metal gray folding chair sinks in the sand next to my cot. I sit slumped over in it, half bent at the waist top, half dead dazed. Quilted mummy-covered face rests on, and is stuck to, the paper covers of the magazines that I opened and tried to read the other day. I try to keep an eye out on the opening to my quiet bungalow, looking to see any mark of time. Its sandy outlook is a misshapen triangle that leads my eye right to the top of where the burn pit would drop in where I dropped in. I wonder if my pink sunglasses are over there. I slide up onto the cot with the plastic and paper and fall asleep. Same o same o.

Corey Major comes in my bungalow and quickly asks me a question. He is my first visitor besides the same daily cast of Dewey the medic, and Driben the driver. Before I get what's going on, he says, Okay, thanks man. I'll return it when I'm done, and walks out with my music. I go back to sleep and wake later in the day just in time to stare at helicopters. Big proper jolly greens. They've arrived as promised. I come out of my shelter. I see all the dudes milling around their rides with their gear. Sgt Wagner is over there somewhere among the silhouettes ready to see his newborn. It could be me, except I told the Major that I wanted to stay and he gave the okay. Going to stay awake, watch them fly away. I wish I was on one just for the fun of a ride cause the Helicopter is one of the best parts of the Army. I stand in the shade, watching the lucky ones standing around their bags. Damn man, it's taking too long. I go back to my cot, and half asleep, listen for the take-off. I think I hear it. My days are quiet, left alone with the wind blowing around me inside my makeshift bungalow.

Five, seven days in? I don't know, feels like ten. I am bored and Dewey's still checking on me. I am better and coming off drugs that aren't working like they used to when I could sleep the boredom away. I start sorting mail, making little stacks here and there, not yet ready for the mass opening. I go back to sleep, but wake up more frequently, and stay awake for longer stretches of time. I end up bored, laying, looking, listening to gaps in between the sucking wind of the rubbery lean-to. It reminds me of being locked inside my own dark isolated beach. I unlock my two nylon green duffel bags that rest in the corner to look for a fresh brown T shirt.

The chair has sunken so far into the sand I dig it out, and move it closer to the door. I'm hungry for action, for interaction, anything besides this protector from the sun. The small lit-opening slaps open by Corey. He steps in and says, Hey fucker, you're finally awake. Dude I missed ya. I came in the other day but you were out of it, so I borrowed your music. I say, Yeah I know dick, there's nothing I could do about it. He says, Yeah I know. Been gone for a couple days, checking bunkers out. Gotta have some tunes. Too bad you're still fucked up. Otherwise your jackass could go with us. I say, Yep. He says, So hey, sorry about taking advantage of you while you were out. Dude, I thought the Flem dog, the Flem Flam was done for. You lucky fucker. Hey man, I got bad news. I broke it. I wasn't paying attention and it got smashed in the back hatch on the track. I feel bad. You're in here all fucked up I'm braking my buddy's shit. Dude, you know how you look right? I say, Yep. He knows this is the only time he can fuck with me. I smile on the inside. He says, Hey Eric, you can't tell anyone. You gotta promise.

I say, I promise. He says, You can't tell anyone, especially Jones. He'll kick my ass. I nod. He says, I got a surprise for ya. You're going to like this. I think, What the fuck is going on with Jones? Corey says, Check this out. I was feeling sorry for ya little ass and I was fucking around in the burn pit. I see different parts of your Oakley's. So I start following this path of pieces around. I didn't have anything to do since we got back, so I put your glasses almost all back together. But I am missing some parts. Dude, I'm sitting in the track thinking I'll go to supply, and see if SSG Dun sun's got anything cool I can scam. Bug him until he gets tired of me. I stand up, pop my head out of the hatch and there they are, just sitting there. Black Oakley's, Razors with the small lens. Someone left them on the 1st Platoon track, and I snatched them. Hey I wanted to tell your jackass sooner, but you're always knocked out like a little bitch.

The big goofy fucker finally figures out the glasses belonged to Jones—the bigger than your usual Filipino dude, who looks more Samoan to me—when he watched Jones looking for his glasses. I like Jones. Fuck it, I'm happy, got a newer pair of used pinkish parted out sunglasses. Going to break out my black sharpie. Corey holds out his opened palm and says, Here man, here's some extra parts. Is it ok if I keep the extra sidepieces? I want to switch my shit out. I say, I don't care, take what ya want. Corey says, Do not tell anyone. I say, Yeah, I'm going to go up to Jones and say, Hey Jones, guess what? You notice anything different about my Oakley's? Corey says, Okay, okay man. Fuck you. I gotta get going. He puts the pieces back in his pocket, and says, Oh hey, I forgot to tell you Sgt Cass is feeling guilty. He confessed he was throwing the used 5-gallon oilcans in the burn pit. He shakes his head. Alright man, I gotta go. I shake my head and think, What the fuck … yeah, what the fuck. I color the frames, put on a new fresh coat. Let them dry. Then fill in the pinholes, gaps of pink color I missed. Finally a different day. Same o same o where ya at?

A couple days later I decide I have to get going on the mail. Read something about some else's life, where they fuck up. Let's see what we can learn from that. I look through the pile of the *Rolling Stone* mags. I may read the month of February. Robin Williams' fear of his own clown. Francis Ford Coppola, I think he's on fire too. Some kind of Apocalypse now. Ah, this is the one. But my reading about his barbecue is cut short, not even close to two pages in. Time to go back and see the medics and the Major this morning.

I get a surprise. The Major tells the medic to wash my face and my hair. She is a pretty blonde. I can appreciate it. The Major has me look at my face for the first time. It's rough and dried, beat-up with scabbed marks dotting my landscape face now. My hair looks like burnt shag carpet. I guess it's not too bad. The Major tells me my face is healing well and I shouldn't have any scaring, but to be really careful of the sun. When I get back to the compound, Dewey asks me about the medic who washed my face and hair. News travels fast. And he continued his comments about the blonde medic after my second run later in the day. Dewey says, Hey, get your hair washed again? Lucky dog!

Another day goes by and I wake up to hang out with myself again. I decide to sit outside, and lean against the track, fresh-faced, unwrapped. I, and the gray folding chair, make a new day of it. Sitting, leaning, reading. Staring in the shade of my day. Got one brown towel draped over my head to shade my new skin from the sneaky, shifting sun. Another towel, rolled tight around my neck, tucked in against the flapping wind and burning sun. I try to keep a step ahead of boredom. What to do next? I am all ready a dried-up, baked twice, getting better, no place to go motherfucker. Sleeping, reading, thinking is my everyday tired.

I see a football arcing past the track, and a figure dashes sideways. It's Dewey, running out for a pass. The football drops into his arms. He and Sgt Tyler are playing catch. I am going to watch these two fuckers run around like goofy shit children. Coppola and his Apocalypse are on hold again. SSG Dun sun shows up. Now that fucker is running around, laughing playing catch. Dewey is talking shit to SSG Dun sun about beating him in a one-on-one football game. The fucking ball is flying back and forth, and I am sitting here like an asshole. Fuck this. I'm going back to helicopters, fires, a jungle and Dennis Hopper. Fucking Dewey's yelling and waving his red freckled white arm at me, Come on, Fleming! Come on, Fleming! I look at them. I shrug and shake my head. It's been almost twelve days since accidentally firebombing myself. Dewey looks to SSG Dun sun. Dewey looks at me. They have three. They need four. They need me.

Now Sgt Tyler is talking shit to SSG Dun sun. They want to prove it to each other. To show what they are saying is true.

Otherwise, it don't mean nothing. It's up to me. No one else around to help these fuckers, to help settle it for today. Dewey and Sgt Tyler say, Come on, Fleming. You and SSG Dun sun against us. I shake my head and hold out the magazine. I can't break my profile. SSG D reminds that if I play, I will be breaking my profile. Yeah, I think about that. Fucking Dewey talking shit and Sgt Tyler talking shit to me, too, that they can beat me and SSG Dun sun. I yell, What if I'm just the Quarterback and let SSGT D be the running back and receiver? They say, Pass only. I say, You can go one-on-one with rushing, or you can go double coverage on SSG Dun sun and with the pass-rush-count. I am the brown-toweled hooded head fool with a final decision for the day. If not today, then when? I guess today, so I step out with my used brown toweled-head ready for some fun. Me and SSG D agree we want to win. They are talking mad shit. SSG Dun sun says, Hey Fleming, I can out run these guys. I know it. He is fast, and always has some left in the tank with a burst of speed. All I have to do is get that ball in front of him as many times as I can. Dewey is constantly screaming and yelling and doing everything he can to distract. He yells, Miss! You're going to miss! When we score, he yells, Goddammit!! When they score, Dewey's like, I told you we gonna win. We score because SSG Dun sun can run wide open. You have to with Dewey and Tyler doing double coverage. They are getting tired. I'm waiting for an opening. Dun sun laughs as he runs. He knows he's going to break free. These two are not in as good of shape, won't be able to hang much longer. I got all the time in the world. Here comes Dewey breaking free, running towards me, leaving SSG D and Sgt Tyler all alone one-on-one. I got to throw it now. We have to keep our lead, keep our score one ahead because we have to win by two. I am the pass rusher for us when Dewey is the quarterback for them. If we score on this pass, we win by two. And so we do. Dewey throws up his hands and says, Ah come on man. Sgt Tyler, you couldn't cover him? We win with laughter. Don't fuck with me and SSG D.

I will show up when needed to win.

How do you describe freedom?

Patrick Ignacio

A lot of people ask Veterans and service members the same question: How do you describe Freedom? Our answer is usually the same, the common: Well, it means different things to different people. Most people do not look at it from our perspective....

We really can't tell you how we describe it. So, I thought that I would share our definition with you and maybe you will be able to see it from our point of view.

First, you have to have a little background about our situation. Imagine, if you will, that you are working at a store making minimum wage. Your manager comes to you and says, There is a man out there in the store, who is armed to the teeth and he said that he will kill the first associate he sees. I need you to go out there and take his weapons and convince him that he should leave the store. What do you say? I can imagine your answer.

Now picture this, you are ten thousand miles from home, and you have not seen your family in eleven months. There is a group of innocent people who are surrounded by heavy fighting and have virtually minutes to live. Your platoon sergeant tells you that the torch for freedom must be carried and you have been chosen to carry it. Your fire team has been tasked with going in, finding them and bringing them to safety. Mind you, these are people you don't know, in a situation you didn't create. Now their lives are in the hands of you and your men.

These "men" as you call them, are between the ages of eighteen and twenty years old. Hell, they cannot even buy a beer. They look to you to guide them in the right direction and to be there to watch their backs. This is exactly what you have sworn to do when you got promoted and took that extra $250.00 a year pay increase. Now you have to tell your men.

In your tent, you brief these "men" about the situation and tell them what your orders are. All they ask is, Who's got point? You tell them to be ready in five. They turn to and gather what they need for the mission. All the time they are doing this they are going through the mental photo album they carry with them and looking at pictures of their wives and kids, parents and siblings. 5 minutes, they are ready.

As you approach the wire, you are laying in the sand scanning the horizon. Nothing. You say to yourself, Pick up the torch. You say to your men, Move out and they do. As you stand and start to move you hear the air around you start to pop, the sand around you erupts in several tiny volcanoes. The mental album comes back for viewing; you push it aside without thinking. You yell over your shoulder, Spread out! You want to scream, Take cover! but you are in a desert and there is none. From behind you, you hear the sound of fresh meat being dropped on the floor, you know what it is, but you cannot stop. You rush to the next sand dune and get really small, almost pushing yourself right into the ground. You scan the horizon, but the heat waves blur anything that is out there. You call for a count, it comes back, and you are down one man. The mental album comes back, and you see the picture of his 19-year-old wife and their new baby that he just showed you yesterday. You say to yourself, Too bad she will never know her dad, he was a great man. That annoying popping noise is back; you slam the album shut and get back to business.

One of your men yells he can see a building; you crawl towards him and ask where. He says right over there, and raises his head to show you. You hear that sound again and watch him go limp; his blood is on your face, and your hands. You instinctively pull him to you and roll him over too late—he has moved to his next mission in guarding the pearly gates of heaven—and you take the radio off his back and put it on. You are down two men now. You make a mental map where they are, and make a vow to return.

You rally what's left of your team and lay out a plan on how to get to the building, hoping it is the right building. You think that if you had some support it might buy you and your men some time and cover to get to the building. You reach the mike on your radio and yell into it, Big Gun, Big Gun, Whisky Tango, over! And you wait.

After what seems like an eternity you hear a crackle on the radio say, Whiskey Tango, Big Gun. Go ahead, over. You give them your coordinates and say, Priority, priority, danger close, over. They respond with, Roger that, get small. Over. You turn to your men and repeat the warning, Get small! You try to become the smallest target you can by getting as flat to the ground as possible.

You hear the whistle in the air and as you feel the impact on the ground, you allow it to lift you up and you are running as fast as you can to the building. You do not look to see if your men are following your lead, you know they are. As you get close to the building, the doors swing open and people are rushing at you, something knocks you to the ground as the building explodes. You cannot hear anything, you try to get up, but nothing is responding. Suddenly you are sliding across the sand, you look up and see two of your men dragging you by your H-harness to the safety of the remains of the building, and the other two are laying down cover fire for you. They look you over, and amazingly you are okay.

Your men look into your face, and using hand signals, they tell you they have found the correct building. You look around and see them yelling to the other two, but you can't hear them. You signal to rally and you make a plan in the dirt. They give you thumbs up to let you know they hear and understand, you just wish you could hear. One of them takes the mike and repeats your last call. The earth shakes and you're up and running again. This time you make it to the building.

Once inside, you post your men and assess the situation; three old men, four women and two young children. The album opens up again and before you can put it away, your last family photo pops up and you see the faces of your little girl. You slam it shut. Mentally you are thinking, One way in, one way out.

Miraculously, your hearing is coming back as one of your own men yells, We are surrounded! You are back in business. You crawl to the one window and slowly rise to see what you are up against; the window explodes in your face sending you and shards of glass flying across the room. Rolling over and dusting yourself off, you huddle your new charges into the far corner and try to smile reassuringly to the children, back to business.

You yell, This is going to get hairy, watch your six! As you crawl back to the window and peek out, you're thinking there is no way out of here. Suddenly there is a frenzy of gunshots and you can hear the bullets hitting the crude concrete causing shards of stone to fly everywhere. In the corner you get on the radio, you tell them you have recovered the target but you are pinned down in the building. They answer back; sit tight, help is on the way. You tell your men. They set up a perimeter and stop anyone from advancing on you. You hear the blades as they chop through the air; you pop smoke and toss it out the window.

The world outside erupts in a deafening sound of gunfire and rockets, the door swings open and you think God himself is standing at the door, but it is just reinforcements who have come to get you out. Everyone grabs your charges and runs for the helos. You make a head count. All accounted for. You feel yourself lifting off; you're in the air, headed for home. You grab the headset and you ask the pilot, What about my men? He knows what you are talking about and replies, It's already done. You check your men and slump to the floor as you listen to the rotor noise start to block out the gunfire and explosions.

Back on the ground, you escort your charges to the aid station and tell your men to go back to the tent. You brief the commander about the mission and go get chow. In the chow line, the man behind the counter asks, Mashed potatoes or stuffing? You reply, What? He says, Your choice. You reply, Mashed potatoes with gravy, thinking to yourself, Now that's freedom.

Freedom has a special flavor the protected will never know....

I Have PTSD … So what?

Patrick Ignacio

I have PTSD or Post Traumatic Stress Disorder. I am one of millions who are affected by it each and every day. Millions of men and women have varying symptoms yet manage to maintain a normal lifestyle. I, along with my cohorts, have been classified as a potential powder keg just waiting on that spark to set us off into a murderous explosion of ire. This is not the case, as I am just as normal as you.

At the end of each and every day, I lay my head down in an attempt to sleep. That in itself is no different than you. But when my eyes close and I should be drifting off into a peaceful bliss, my mind takes over, and I am tormented in my dreams with a vivid and exaggerated version of every combat encounter witnessed. There has been nary a night that I do not experience this, and I have not had an uninterrupted night of sleep for years. Yet in the morning, I rise with the consistency of the sun, roll out of my sweat soaked bed, and shake off the remnants of the nightly battles and start my day … just like you.

I am functional in society, but I am a little more vigilant than you. I am always on the lookout for danger, avoiding large crowds and loud places. But somehow, I can still manage to go out to eat, shop for my clothes and drive my car. I pay close attention to those around me. I see the drug deal that just took place on my right and notice the people who just don't belong in a certain situation. You may not have evil intentions, but I will notice nonetheless.

I have guns and weapons. As a matter of fact, I just about always have one on me. Or at least I used to have one on me at all times, especially when I went to the shooting range. You see, even though I have PTSD, I am still a Sheepdog watching out for my flock. I don't brandish my weapon and most of the time you won't even know I have it on my body, but it is there. I also used to carry a large knife in my pocket, one that could cause serious injury or death if used improperly, or used properly in self-defense. Now that I have a wife and a young daughter, I simply carry a pen and my keychain with me all the time. I have never used any of my weapons in a malicious manner and I never will, but in my duties as a Sheepdog I will not hesitate to draw down on you should the circumstance warrant it. I may be armed, but I am not dangerous.

There are times when I am extra medicated. My PTSD comes in cycles and when things get bad I need that extra chemical push to regulate me. I accept this and because of it, I do not drink alcohol or coffee or even caffeine-free anything. I have other physical problems that could easily warrant an addiction to painkillers, but just like most of us with PTSD, I avoid them.

I have never committed violence in the workplace or in public, just like the vast majority of those who suffer with me. My co-workers as well as family and friends know I spent time in the military but they do not know of my daily struggles, and they won't because I don't want to burden them. When I was working I could still communicate with my subordinates and supervisors in a very clear and concise manner. Up to this point, I have not gone berserk or "really" threatened anybody around me. I have never physically assaulted anyone out of anger or rage.

It pains me when I listen to the news, and every time a veteran commits a crime (or commits suicide) their action is automatically linked to, and blamed on PTSD. Yes, there are some who cannot control their actions due to the wounds in our souls, the imbalance in our heads, the injuries in our bodies, but don't put a label on us as if we are all incorrigible. Very few of us are bad. There are more of us out there who are trying harder to do well than the lesser alternative.

Do not pity me. I know who I am and recognize the journey that has shaped me into who I am. I have no regrets about anything that I have done in the past and look forward to many wonderful years in the future, most especially, since I have a loving wife and beautiful daughter. I freely take every step of life during the day, knowing that there is something that will haunt me at night.

You're in the Army Now

Terre Fallon Lindseth

I know this sounds ridiculous. But I really didn't realize that I had joined the "Army" when I raised my hand and swore to protect the Constitution from all Enemies Foreign and Domestic.

The simple answer is I blame my mother.

It was all her idea.

In fact it was at her insistence that I met with the recruiters—she never mentioned the word Army—who very conveniently came to her bar, sat on stools, smiled at me and told me how fun it is to be in the National Guard.

The National Guard! They wear a uniform one weekend a month and hang out at the local big grey building with lots of jeeps in the parking lot. My recruiter told me that for two weeks every summer they go to summer camp. I had been to a summer camp once in the third grade, and I really liked it. So going every summer for two weeks and getting paid for it sounded good to me.

You think like that when you are barely 17, and don't really understand the details of what's being said, or even the big picture of what's being presented.

I really did not understand my mother's insistence on me joining the National Guard. Of course, hindsight and a 20/20 view from almost 40 years could tell me a lot. My mother? Not so. I asked her not too long ago why she wanted me to join the military, and she replied, "Oh, I don't know."

So maybe the question should be: "Why did I join?"

Looking back, I think I joined because after quitting high school on my 16th birthday, getting a rotten job on the graveyard shift, moving into my own apartment, and graduating from High School one night after passing all of the required exams, my quest to be an adult looked rather shapeless.

So when those nice recruiters told me the National Guard would pay 75% of my college tuition, something suddenly changed in me. It was like the pride I felt when the nameless Principal at a high school I never attended shook my hand and congratulated me for graduating high school. The possibility of actually going to college because the National Guard would pay for most of it, and all I had to do was wear a uniform one weekend a month and go to summer camp ... well, I think that was the clincher.

My mother drove me to the armory to take the entrance exam. I got a high score the nice recruiter said, and I qualified to go to school to become an officer. *Oh that's nice,* I thought. They then had me talk to a nice woman in one of those uniforms who told me how fun boot camp was and for her the best part of being in the National Guard was going away to summer camps.

Everyone was very nice and welcoming. We were all on first name basis. Alice, the woman I was talking with, had me sign a stack of papers. My mother had to sign the papers, too, because I was under 18. Bob, the nice recruiter, said the only thing left to do was to swear me in. I entered an office where a serious man told me to raise my hand and repeat after him. I became serious because he was serious. I repeated the words and felt the weight of them. He shook my hand.

When I told my friends that I had joined the National Guard and I was going to go to boot camp, they were surprised, maybe even amused. I was the last person they would ever imagine joining the military. My group of friends at that time consisted of working class spawn whose expectation of life was, get a job, hate it, quit it, get another job. Continue this until you realize you really need a job and then settle into one for the rest of your life. Marry because it's the thing to do, have children and bumble through parenting, divorce, remarry, etc.

For us, reaching beyond that scope of life was discouraged because it was too scary, failure being inevitable. Anyone trying for a better life was seen as rejecting the others, trying to be "better" than the rest. A snob.

My friends kept telling me how hard it would be and that I had better practice my push-ups. I could sense their anticipation that I would fail and come home. I could almost hear their contempt.

Well I wasn't worried. I would make it through. What did they know? I was going to boot CAMP!

A couple of months went by before I received a letter informing me of my date to go to camp. There was also a packing list enclosed. I didn't need to bring much, but did have to buy 10 white cotton underwear and 4 bras. That was a big cost for me, because I was definitely a pink, red, or black panty girl.

I don't remember who took me to the airport. I know it wasn't a family member. There was no big send off, but I do remember being thrilled. I was going on an adventure. It was my second time on a plane, and after missing my connecting flight in Chicago because I didn't realize I had to change terminals, I got on a much later flight, and arrived in South Carolina well after midnight. A uniformed man was standing by the luggage turnstile. He told me to get on the green bus. The bus was full of tired travelers. It rolled us through the night for what seemed an endless journey.

Then it appeared. A massive other world. We passed through a gate into an ugly industrial complex of gray block buildings and bright streetlights. The men were emptied from the bus first, leaving me and one other girl. We sat in silence as the males collected their bags and shuffled off into one of the block buildings. Our bus finally trundled on. We stopped at another block building. We were met by a curt young woman who simply said, "Grab your bags and follow me."

We followed her into the concrete gray building and up four flights of stairs. We passed through double swinging doors into a massive bay of a room. The only light inside the room was from the streetlights shining through the windows. There were beds lined up against the walls on both sides, with sleeping forms in them. There must have been twenty beds on either side. We were directed to two beds across from us. We quietly grabbed what was needed from our suitcases and crawled into bed. My mind was on an electric buzz of fatigue and worry. I was sleeping in the middle of 40 strangers moaning, snoring, making body sounds. And I thought to myself, *What is this place?*

The morning came too soon and violently. I heard voices and movement, and as they became louder I hunkered down in my bed and covered my head with the pillow. A screaming voice pierced my sleep, and I looked up to see an angry face hovering over me. "Get up now!" "Why are you screaming at me?" I asked. "Get your ass out of bed NOW!" I sat up and said to the angry woman, "Look we just got here at three in the morning, you cannot possibly expect us to get up so early." Angry woman screamed, "You have 10 minutes to get in formation and move to the chow hall!" "Oh," I replied, "go ahead without me. I'll join you after breakfast." And I flopped back on my bunk and covered my head with my blanket.

The blanket was no protection from the pain of her screaming voice within one inch of my ear. I popped up to protest more when I heard, "You have zero eight minutes until formation" from her retreating form. Looking around, I saw 40 women dressed, with made beds. I got up.

Formation consisted of 40 some women trying to stand next to each other in a square blob. We were yelled at, and walked what seemed like miles to a huge block building surrounded by a single file line. We were placed in the line and instructed how to stand (with our hands behind our backs, knees locked, looking straight ahead) while waiting. It was there, in that moment, standing in line behind hundreds of others with my arms aching that I decided I didn't like this shit.

Once inside the building it was a grand central station of people, tables, noise of clanking metal, and scrapping chairs, but not voices. There were lines everywhere. The effort to orientate was dizzying. So I just followed the person in front of me into a long line toward what looked like food at the end of it. I grabbed my metal tray and step-by-step approached the servers who spooned food on my metal tray, no questions asked. I now had to find a table to sit at. I couldn't look for someone I recognized to join because I didn't know anyone. So I looked out at the thousands of tables and hoped to find an empty chair. I set my tray down at an empty place and went to get a drink. All I could manage was to go to the nearest drink island, which only offered lemonade or Kool-Aid. I settled for a glass of red Kool-Aid, then back to my table, and that took some looking.

Ah, food! I was ready to eat. I started with the scrambled rubber eggs, then a bite of cardboard bacon, cold toast, drink of sugar Kool-Aid, and then I put my fork in the mound of white stuff. I didn't recognize it. I took a small taste and there was none. No taste. So I looked at the person next to me and asked, "What is this?" The person next to me looked down at his plate as if to avoid being exposed. I then asked the other people at the table, "Does anyone know what this is?" And then from behind me came a screaming voice. "There is no talking in the mess hall, recruit! Grab your tray and exit immediately!" "What?" I demanded. "I just want to know what this is! I'm not finished eating!" The voice screamed again and I was forced to pick up my tray, escorted by both an obnoxious yelling person and my own embarrassment.

After dumping my tray, I stood outside waiting while the rest of my group finished their breakfasts. My entire being was possessed with a foul mood of the unfairness, homesickness, regret, and rebellion.

We marched back to our barracks and our "room" where we were to be given instructions on the proper military way to make our bunk. Everything was okay until the screech of displeasure rended the air. The small Corporal, who was my tormenter, fouled the air with her disbelief that my bed was not made. I tried to remind her that she only gave me eight minutes to be outside, and besides, we were suppose to learn *how* to make a bed so what difference did it make?

In that moment I became the outsider. I felt every woman in the room distancing herself from me. I was on my own. The Corporal went verbally ballistic; I became the prop of how to make a bed, and how to properly respond to questions, and how to do a proper push-up. Later in the day I demonstrated how to "police" the field of trash.

My first week at the reception station was not encouraging. No one wanted to hear that I had joined the National Guard, not the Army. And most of my fellow recruits kept their distance from me out of self-preservation. They understood shut-up, keep your head down, don't stand out. But I had no such filter of course. My mouth and attitude were my company, along with my best friend, self-righteousness.

The week was a series of long lines and walking (now called marching), to gather and learn to wear our personal "issue." Like ugly green clothes that made us look pregnant with thick thighs. Boots that were stiff and biting, and were made for men. (My boots were size four.) Green wool socks that itched and scratched and made life hell in the South Carolina heat. All of this stuffed in a duffle bag that smelled of diesel oil. Trips to and from the lines, back to the barracks to offload our newly issued items. Lines for blood drawing, finger prints, name tags. Lines inside, lines outside. Everyday a personal experience of this impersonal institution. No one knows you; no one wants to know you because in a few days you are off to basic training. Where, they tell you, it will be a lot harder than it is here. The lines then concluded with us dressed up in our new Class A jackets with hats and marched through the heat, one by one, to get our official military pictures taken.

For me that first week was hell. If I thought I hated school and its rules, I had a new understanding of hate. My bad attitude was my only source of intimacy. I was disappointed, pissed off, and well, trapped. I was tormented by that Corporal, that little sparrow of a young woman who was full of herself and heady with the self-importance of being in charge of 40 some women. All the other women seemed impressed. Not me. I saw her as a little cock. I mean, we had just learned the ranks and she was just a Corporal. Never mind I had no rank on my collar. I was a private, E1, not even with a mosquito wing. I was the lowest of the low.

The little cocky Corporal was warming up to some of the women in the group. I guess it's lonely at the top. She held court, sharing stories of basic training and what they could expect. They listened with rapt attention as if this knowledge would give them a leg up in basic. I of course, would never join that group. There was no way I would ever show her an ounce of admiration. So I listened with half an ear, from a distance demanded by the smoking section.

What a menagerie of the female species. All colors, all sizes, every regional accent. It was interesting and scary at the same time. I had come from Nebraska. Lily-white Nebraska. I had never really known anyone who was not white, not in person. Here was a mix of white, black, brown. They were young, and not so young. They came in every size. Tall, short, extremely short, thin, stick thin, chunky, curvy, big breasted, flat chested, big hips, no hips. Some were mothers, all were daughters. They were city girls, country girls, Yankees, Southerners, Midwesterners, Alaskans.

Who were these women? Why did they join? That question was answered every time they uttered an uneducated or undereducated phrase. They were poor. They were desperate for something better in their lives. They were desperate for something different than what life had doled out to them. There was a sense that there was one thing to do in this place. Survive. Make it through. That was the feeling from the majority of the girls. It was one of the reasons I was on my own. They had a goal to make it through and onto something important to them. I was not committed to anything important, just my complaint about being in the wrong place. This was their place. This was their chance.

There was a handful of college educated amongst us. They kept to themselves. They were older and already wore the rank of Private First Class, and had a different energy that exuded a desire to thrive.

They were going to be successful. They weren't going to be like the others. It was an intriguing difference.

One girl I remember was from Mississippi. She had the worst hair and teeth I had ever seen. Her Afro hair was straight down to her ears and dry as straw. It looked like it would crack off if brushed. Her front teeth were extremely bucked and had a wide gap. She was stick thin; her skin was the color of a dark plum. I was amazed at her tiny proportions. Her waist was so small they couldn't find clothes or field gear to fit; she had narrow hips and long legs. To me she seemed like a gazelle. I never heard her speak. I liked her instantly, and I wanted her to make it.

Of course in every group of women there is the mother figure. We had many. One was a large black woman, who moved with extreme confidence and superiority. When she walked down the bay she expected others to move out of her way. She collected subordinates. She held court during our down time, giving advice and encouragement. At night she would braid hair for the black girls. I thought she needed to be seen, to be important.

The woman who bunked next to me, the one who arrived when I arrived, was from New Jersey. We liked each other, and helped each other figure out our new clothes and field gear. I cracked up every time she spoke. I thought her accent was so tough sounding. She was short, and extremely muscular. Her hair was dark and cut short and spiky. She was streetwise, and that was an attribute in the military, instead of the liability it was in civilian life.

As with any big group, cliques formed in our group of forty. Little islands of women, all clustered by type. I didn't join any clique. No one wanted to hear my persistent complaint that I was really in the National Guard. So I kept to myself, trying to adjust to the fact that I had been duped. I was in the Army, and the only way to get through this was to get with the program, and surrender my self-righteous complaint, leaving it at the door. Because once I got through this I could go home, and all I had to do was one weekend a month and summer camp.

Of course, forty of us had to brush our teeth, use the toilets and take showers, clique or no clique. To accommodate this the Army provided us four trough sinks each with four faucets, eight stalls with toilets, ten urinals, and one massive concrete room with multiple shower heads along the walls and on top of poles in the middle of the room. It was your middle school PE shower nightmare all over again.

The first couple of days some women would get up early to do their hair and make-up. Some would shower after midnight. Some did a kind of body wash at the sink while wearing robes because they had not built up the nerve to shower with others. By the third day, after hours of marching and sweating in the South Carolina heat in new boots that bit and blistered, and field gear that rubbed your back raw, the shower became a beckoning oasis.

Stripped of our uniforms and airs, the shower told a deeper story. It told of feminine beauty, frailty, and strength, and the will to achieve. It showed birth from cesarean scars and stretch marks. It told of abuse from scars that should not be where they were. It exposed tattoos of rebels and lovers. It displayed athletic limbs, long graceful muscles, round tummies, hips and asses. It washed blood from heavy periods down the drains. In this Goddess steam room we were one, bonded by the aches of our muscles and the love of a good smelling shampoo.

As the week went on, the bay began to reek of BENGAY, the moaning sounds made by the desperately tired, and the night music from the muted sounds of crying. Homesickness had swept through like a virus. Confidence had evaporated like water in a birdbath under the South Carolina sun. Brief moments of mixed laughter and misery were shared when someone would cry out in the night, "I need my man! Lord, I need my man!" And then someone yelled out the obvious, "I can't believe I'm in the Army!" To which I yelled, "Welcome to my fucking club!" And the whole bay burst out laughing, and for the first time I felt part of the whole, as we all surrendered to exhaustion.

Right before we were to leave the reception center we had to clean our "bay." We were ordered to push all of the bunks and lockers to one end of the bay so that we could mop and wax the polished cement floor. Once dry, we all took a turn at the waxing machine. The waxing machine like everything else was gray. It was a large industrial beast with a big round cylinder at the bottom that sat on pink bristles. A round tube protruded up from the cylinder and was topped with straight handlebars. The beast had a long tail of a cord plugged into the wall.

No one knew how to use the machine, but we all thought we could.

One by one we took hold of the machine only to be thrown

off balance by it once it was turned on and its power unleashed. It should be easy, we thought. We just needed to push it or pull it but that pushing and pulling caused the 200 lb. machine to go off balance and dance on one side, pulling our weight with it. It fell over and quivered with roaring menace, scaring us all into screaming with glee. No one wanted to approach it. So we unplugged it to turn it off. It took four of us to set it up straight again.

One by one we tried to succeed. Some approached the machine with confidence, some with wariness. One by one we failed. We all laughed and encouraged the next to try, secretly hoping she would do no better, and she didn't. It was a long process of elimination, until we had all failed. Then a training sergeant took the machine in hand and ran it smoothly over the floor with just her fingertips on the handles. She explained that the machine hovers and all we have to do is guide it with a very light touch. Trying to control the machine works against its design and causes chaos. The trick was to understand its design.

For many in the group what the training sergeant said was just training on how to work a machine. For me it was a metaphysical lightning bolt. The machine was life. Perfectly designed for ease and only requiring the light touch of guidance. Unfortunately, most of us try to control it. It was a great lesson, one I relearned many times.

The morning to ship out from the reception center to our basic training companies arrived on a wave of anxiety and worry. I thought it was useless, and personally, I was ready to get the hell out of the reception center. We were warned about how mean the drill instructors were going to be and had a picture of cannibals drilled into our imaginations. And even though I was still wallowing in my disappointment of joining the Army, all I wanted to do was get on with it, whatever that meant.

We were all sitting on our duffle bags that had our names and social security numbers stenciled on them, baking in the southern sun. A huge, loud, gassy monster like something out of a Sci-Fi movie rumbled towards us. Our conveyance had arrived. It was a gigantic semi-cab about two stories high, with a ladder on the side for the driver to climb up to get in. It had a 12-foot arm stretched out grabbing onto the Titanic behind it. There was a big gap between the cab and the trailer. I had never seen anything like it.

Not even in *Star Wars*. We were told to climb in the gaping back end.

We shuffled over, dragging our duffle bags and suitcases; we helped each other lift our bags into the hold at the rear. I imagined we looked like refugee immigrants boarding a ship to the unknown world. Some were crying to relieve stress; most of us were in stunned silence. The inner bowel of the trailer was hot, and the windows were too high to see out of. We had to slide down wooden benches to make way for the next woman until we were packed in, shoulder-to-shoulder, hip-to-hip.

We had no idea what direction we were going or what the landscape looked like. After a week in a concrete prison block we were now in the belly of a whale. A hot, stinky whale that belched when the brakes were released. No one said a word as we trundled along, and our sweaty bodies danced in unison at every pothole, turn or stop. It felt like we were animals being shipped off to slaughter.

It is imaginable that I was questioning once again my presence in the Army. But in truth, the situation was so foreign, so unknowable that my mind was completely blank. My only desire was to get out of that stifling beast.

When we finally came to a full stop and the doors were thrown open, the blinding sun hit us with a hurricane of angry voices yelling at us to "Get off!" "Move!" "Grab your gear! Get moving!" We dismounted with the quickness that only comes in your dreams of running through quick sand. Lethargy gripped our dehydrated bodies and stunned minds, and chaos reigned as we unskillfully shuffled down the benches to the rear and grabbed at bags before hopping down from the trailer piling on top of each other. The faster we tried to get out of the trailer the more we bottlenecked and careened into each other. It was a mass of women and bags piled up on the ground at the door opening, with a line of women inside the trailer attempting to move forward to get off.

The Drill Instructors barked and harassed and allowed us to fumble in our chaos until they intervened to move things along.

I was off the trailer bent over trying to get a grip on my duffle and suitcase when I realized the person yelling was yelling at me. "What are you doing here?" Now that was the fucking question of the year, wasn't it? And I had just gotten off the trailer and it was obvious already to a Drill Instructor that I didn't belong. Well, maybe NOW we can get this National Guard thing straightened out! "Gilly, answer me! What are you doing here?" I stood up and came face to with a very black, sweaty, and serious man. "Gilly, what are you doing here?" Gilly? My mind seemed to be registering something was strange. The DI looked at me like he would bore a hole through me. He looked hopeful, like seeing a long lost friend. Again he demanded, "Gilly, what are you doing here?" I did a little look to my left and then to my right, no Gilly there. I was by myself. I looked at the DI and said, "I'm Fallon."

Excerpts – Behind the Razor Wire

Kenneth James

You have heard of the L.Z.

Putting it together

Since 2003 maybe

You have also heard of behind the wall

You have, haven't you?

Are you in touch with the unknown war?

I'm lonely in it

Constitutional rights denied

And the other unknown war

Stenched

Behind the razor wire

Where innocence is thieved

From a Marine

Yes, Marines are innocent, too

I'm lonely in it

behind the razor wire

stenched

with not a hand to hold

Yes, Marines need SUPERHEROES

in the lack of advocacy

am I finally finding it

will I find it at all

or will it always be too hard to grasp?

I feel lonely in it

Stenched

They call themselves peckerwoods, and other miscreants do as well, I call them fecal woods. Piles of it in here, behind the razor wire, the cinderblocks filled with rebar and cement. Nope, digging out of prison stops here. Some of the prisons even have electric fences, maybe all of them do, and they definitely have guard towers with guards who are being punished for bad behavior, and other guards who don't want any other responsibility except for watching the grounds all day. There were even gun towers in chow hall at Tracy, the gladiator school. A menacing looking guard aims the fully automatic weapon at various people when they walk in, like he is ready to shoot them, or me, or somebody. Anybody.

This also exacerbated my depressed state, where I became more disoriented from mental anguish, and being severely victimized. I was hopeless and helpless to do anything, or to find anybody who would, or could do anything in order to get justice. I was just turning 34, and it was all over for me because some dumb-assed cunt wanted to feign her innocence and refused to tell the truth of what exactly happened. She pursued me. I did not pursue her. She did not even want to think about the truth. She was illegally influenced, and that influence became her out to not speak about the truth of what really happened. For example, at the time of the court proceedings, she was about five months pregnant by one of her adult sex partners. And no, I was not the father. I was never one of her sex partners. She drowned herself in the illegal influence of her mother, her father who was a prison guard, and her uncle.

Guard Hancock is the orchestrator of crimes against me, he is a …

He wishes that his crimes would all be forgotten. He said that god will judge it all in the end. He is fine with the crimes he already committed against me, and never having to be accountable for them. After I was subjected to false imprisonment, and 3 years of additional torment on parole, he wrote me a note, a phone text that said: *I forgave you, now you have to forgive me.* What does he need my forgiveness for? Maybe it lies in the facts of that he tried to have me murdered.

Guard Hancock put into motion the green light on my life in the jails and prisons. These were his playgrounds, and he was going to make damned sure he would not be found out for the crimes he committed[s] against me. He was going to see me dead, and it would have been the best crime that he would ever have gotten away with. It came VERY CLOSE to happening 3 times ... I was minutes from death ... and many many other times death was right around the corner. But Death never found me, not in the sense of a dirt-nap. I am a Marine with street smarts and I saw it coming. It wasn't as some people told me: It was not my time to go; God has a plan for your life; you were very lucky; how did you survive that; I could not have lasted one day of what you have been through; God will not put you through more than you can handle; etc.

So besides not feeling crazy, but driven crazy from all of the Bullshit victimization, and murdered by lies, by the crimes that were committed as a result of those lies, here I was inside the ugliest facility. I was behind the razor wire.

The drive
  a dude named Gnomes
  trying to dog me out
  too complex
  no light on him
  not just the mad dogging
  lies begat lies
  amplifying focus on unrealities
  I'm lonely in it
  the torment beating my ass all the way
  smelling the metal of the benches,
  the oil of the tires,
  evaporating air being sucked up by predators all around
  and me
  the pavement shut out from the slamming of the doors

The processing

In-take

The fenced in area all by myself

The first cell and the first person I was stuck with
in processing was the crackhead, and the stories....

The second young man who was falsely imprisoned

out of association and hanging with the wrong crowd....

and then being Processed to the prison

they kept me there in Tracy

It was different once I was transferred to Tracy forever

The voices and the sounds and the smells

The first prisoner in that prison

The second prisoner ...

and me

Behind the razor wire, the electric fences, the wall, cinder blocks reinforced by rebar, and the monsters, all the monsters.

10 years behind the razor wire ... celled up with 100 persons maybe 40. But, is there a difference when you are jam-packed into a 6x10 foot space? And these monsters are not just the only ones who are shoved into this container with you. The monsters are everywhere, with various uniforms, and various faces and characteristics of deception. You may see someone well dressed, and speaking extremely well, with fragrances of the finest perfumes or colognes. They are the same in any other uniform; they may have the best hair day, well groomed, and good looking. In prison, the monsters are not just the prisoners, they are Guards, Wardens, Medical Tech. Assistants, Sergeants, Lieutenants, Captains, and the prisoners, some prisoners, most prisoners, the Psychs, the Social Workers, the Doctors, and the mother-fucking fecal wood cockroaches!

At any given time, you may not be able to recognize just who is a monster and who is not. It may be difficult for you to see and recognize the hidden devil's vile filth that is just as deep as it may be in the scraggliest disheveled monstrosities oozing with a stench. The unrecognizables are no different than the loud and ear piercing filth spewing from their mouths. Each monster equips themselves with their own individual tactics to infiltrate and destroy their target.

For those of us who are squeezed into these tiny containers, cells as they are called, when we put the rack down, we are either 2 inches away from the person in the next rack, or you are above ... in an upper lower situation where you are approximately 4 feet above or below the person in either rack. Either way, once the door closes, you are stuck, and if you are with a homicidal maniac or any kind of criminal who is always in their predacious state, it may be too late for you before the door is opened to stop the chaos. Fact is, nobody may know someone is dead or dying until the next day. And, that is just one real scenario for the everyday when one is locked into this tiny space with god knows whom.

Behind the RAZOR WIRE – Besides jail, the first location where I existed for over a year was at Deuel Vocational Institution. This place was gladiator school – DVI was a receiving prison from many of the local jails. Inside these cells was an upper and lower bunk bed, with maybe 2½ feet between the bunk and the wall. In this one, there was a desk on the wall in the middle. Some had a sliver of a window if you were on the outside wall, but when on the inside wall, there was no window. In this hellhole of a dungeon, the walls were all painted putrid dingy dark greenish brown with a little dim-lit 10, or 15-watt bulb above each bunk.

The cell doors are spring loaded in these cells at gladiator school. They slam so hard, as if warning you that if your limbs are caught between the steel door and the steel frame, your fingers or hand or arm will be severed. They also will at anytime just pop open, which could easily be the day that you will also be murdered by the criminals/monsters that will rush in to kill you. In the gated cage across the 3 tier steel stairways, the guard who is also imprisoned—at least for his shift minus breaks—operates the control switch. Every once in a while, someone will throw someone over the rails from the third tier onto the concrete or the steel tables set for four. Some of the stools are missing their round steal seats, and the sharp steel square posts just wait to catch a head, or another body part that will be impaled or severed.

Oh, and there is a t.v., way down at the other end of the hall, the place you can go out to "socialize" with all the people you have always wanted to socialize with. Maybe, that is, if you are a homie who dabbles in the seedy ways of life, or worse, if you are full on into the inanity of thievery of anything that is not yours, including but not limited to—the lives of others.

Just make an attempt to watch some media, before the next fight, the next riot, or until some criminals come at you to get you to join their "team." Before they come at you with the inanity talk, "Yo homie, what U in for?" They are not trying to be your friend, nor are they curious. It is much more cynical than that. It is not really a team of course,

it is a gang,
it is initiation,
it is manipulation,
it is sex slavery,
it is the punk ass bitches owned by that group, maybe for life,
maybe for the duration of prison time,

whether or not they get you to join their "team" depends upon how strong the mind is of the person who is facing the violence and threat of violence. Oh, you will get another number, their #. You will get another name, and a bunch of other shit will all be written on your skin. You will be inked for life, maybe from head to toe, and not in the good way. Not the artsy-fartsy way that people for generations have done, including Marines, and the other military branches that serve Our Great Nation. No, this is a part of prison politics, the manipulation by control freak recidivists. The recidivists are the monsters who are, and who are not, paying for their crimes. And these prison politics are the destruction for any hope of civility. The civility that is desperately needed when you are nonexistent, and existing in hell's dungeons. The civility of caring compassionate visitors, which I had. Or the civility of an advocate with the working knowledge to secure justice for me, which I didn't have.

So, if you were, as I was, falsely imprisoned, you would constantly be more than annoyed at the way things are done in prison. You would be hard pressed to find people who had courtesy, who were considerate, who understood logic and reasoning. That kind of normalcy did not exist. I looked, but could not find it. I began to notice that I had become a ghost that was visited, that was spoken to, that was ordered around and victimized, everyday, victimized.

Nonetheless, if you could find someone who could be your advocate, or a friend, someone who loved you, or even just liked or accepted you, it is only your ghost they would be seeing. Like my ghost you see today, if you have ever seen it. If you haven't seen it, look closer, and see the nature between the living and the dead. This is my hell of being falsely imprisoned. I turned into a ghost ... just wishing I could live again. And guess what—10 years out now, and still I'm not living. I am still a ghost.

At DVI I wasn't ever allowed to pick someone to cell with. I hardly made it out. I did not want to mingle. I did not want to talk to anybody. It was more than hell. At the other prison, you rarely would get to pick your own cellie (a term I have never used, but be my guest). Most prisoners were criminals of one degree or another. You would never know what kind of criminal they were except for their behavior.

Some were no longer criminals at all,
some repented,
some were sorry,
some were making a new identity for themselves,
some made amends from the regret that haunted them

Oh, but the warden had teams of guards putting that shit together,
classifying criminal records,
saying what a prisoner was,
the hierarchy of crimes
putting hits on their heads,
setting up the criminal cartel.

This is the shit they put on me

sex criminal
child predator
repeat offender
monster

all from what they thought was true
all from the allegations
all from the court transcriptions
all not true
all from the phone calls from guard hancock
all from what they read
all from their corrupt practices
all from the lack of reality
all not true

and other guards, staff, and prisoners
would then make up more of their own
all not true

It doesn't matter what their motives were, the guards, staff, and prisoners falsely judged me, and they used their judgments to justify the crimes they committed against me. There are many people looking forward to committing crimes against the accused, whether they are rightfully imprisoned or falsely imprisoned.

It is a system of the predacious.

Predacious criminals would threaten suicide in order to go to these suicide watch prisons, which became hubs where they would pass notes and reconnect with other homies, or in order to commit crimes on a specific target. They also would use the hub to be relocated to another prison in order to be able to hit other specific targets.
In the one hundred and twenty four months I was behind the razor wire, I was at 2 prisons, except when I was on suicide watch. In the

other prisons I was isolated. Most of the time, they still managed to torture and torment me. There was only maybe one prison where maybe a couple of the staff actually seemed to care about my well-being.

It's a system of complex politics.

Such a nurturing culture ... no really, hear my facetiousness. No really, hear my seriousness. I loved civility. But in most cases, it was non-existent.

it was stench
not only does the stench kill you,
stuffed into a single cell
so many other men,
not regular men,
those who committed crimes
those accused of crimes
those looking to commit more crimes
stench on top of stench
and you are stuck there sitting,
most likely standing,
numb
you cannot move
there is no room to move
you can't move,
your eyes shift to various different places
to other eyes that are shifting
if only for a moment to gauge
to where the stench is coming from
the double stench of those who are in there—
the stench of stink
the stench of the criminal minds.

Writing this, I can't get to it from here. I just keep trying, but I skirt the issues, troubling me....

So, I am a Marine in Gladiator school. Being a Marine only means that the predacious recidivists may not murder you as quickly.

Every time a door opens, or you come up to a doorway, or another hallway, and even to your container ... you better be aware, especially if you are a target.

I was and still am, a target, a POW, the MIA, of a war obscured within the threads of California's corrupt judicial system.

Gladiator school was the first year, where death hung around every corner. I was brought here in handcuffs and shackles on a 2 ½ hour trip with the vile fucks that rode in the back of the van, the guards in the front, and me.

Gnomes started spreading falsities about me, covering up the sick piece of shit he is, and maybe doing favors for the guards as well. It was 3 jails and 4 months after the shams of the court's judicial processes and all the crimes committed against me. It was only four months, but it seemed like lifetimes of torment, and it only continued with the same and greater intensities.

By the time I was subjected to jail that ended in criminal court proceedings ... it was 7 days of suicide watch ... it was crazies yelling and screaming crazy shit all day and all night long ... it was lights on all day and night ... it was shit, piss, and cum on the walls ... it was a plastic coated whatever it was ... some called it a mattress ... this thing that was 2 inches of nothing wrapped in plastic ... set on a steel sheet with the same piss, shit and cum on it as well ... it was stench ... it was ... it ... it ...

was lonely in it

behind the razor wire

The Old Soldier

Erren Geraud Kelley

The Old Soldier
holds his rifle, though it doesn't
exist anymore
at night, his thousand yard stare
pierces toward heaven
as he slowly walks toward
his long goodbye

mama's whippings toughened him
for 'nam
he became the warrior,
he didn't want to be

his smile disarmed anyone
like a word or a handshake
years ago, he started saying his
long goodbye

he was there, but not all there
he wished he could drive his
sports car again or hold
a girl, as a motown tune wails
wished she could share a long
goodbye

he takes one look at the horizon,
he gave his all for god and country
he was the savior, they didn't deserve
but it was his home, too
a gleam still lingers in his eyes
as he takes each step towards
a long goodbye

Private Kenner gets chow

Adam Cloys

We came back in from the field before sunset, ready to start the long weekend. This had been a good exercise for my squad. Everyone seemed motivated to finish up by Thursday and not have to report back until Tuesday morning PT formation.

By the time it was all the way dark we began to realize we would not be released early or even any time soon. Most of the company was gathered at the dock behind the orderly room where a safety brief would eventually take place.

My company is dismantling and re-cleaning weapons that were already re-cleaned, re-checked and re-double-checked. Not all of Brigade HQ is back in from the field. Of course they won't start tearing down until all the Battalions report returning safely.

Our Company will not be dismissed until our Battalion is dismissed. Our Battalion is not dismissed before our Brigade is dismissed. We're longing for that safety briefing to begin.

Staff Sergeant King is my immediate supervisor. He asks me, "Did Kenner get chow?"

This trick question is both loaded and rhetorical because the answer is probably no, although there is no way I can know that yet. Private Kenner is one of my guys, but the past week or so I have begun to get used not having to look after him.

Thank god fucking "Ken Doll" got stuck on rear "D" this time. I wonder how much easier some squads have it without a piece of work like him to make everyone else have to compensate for. He can't be issued a weapon now that he's been involved in two domestic disputes on file with the MPs.

Private Kenner's wife, Allyse, had beaten his ass in both cases. Not only was she unharmed but she freely admits he never put a finger on her. Still, he's been living it up on rear "D" working in the orderly room getting showers and hot chow at the DFAC every day.

The rest of us haven't showered for over a week. Not a big deal. You can smell how clean Kenner is though. He has not eaten, of course. He had an opportunity before the DFAC closed but he skipped it because, and I quote, "I thought we might get released early."

Private Kenner does not resemble a Ken Doll. I think the guys all call him that for his Ken-Doll-like brains. They might mean it in the way big guys get named Tiny. Either way, suddenly he's mine to look after again, to "follow up" with.

We leave Kenner and take SSG King's car to run a few other errands. Our M-16s are locked up in Sergeant King's trunk. It isn't exactly legal to ride around Post like that but our arms room isn't accepting anyone's weapons yet. We have starving guys to look after, what else can we do?

We should be marching in formations while signed for our M-16s, but Fort Hood is really huge so we decided to drive anyway.

Behind the passenger seat where I'm sitting are the buckets of Popeye's Chicken we're talking back to my highly deserving guys who are still cleaning rifles behind the orderly room. We also have chicken for "Ken Doll."

We're stopped outside SSG King's house. He has on-Post housing and he's running in for some two liter Pepsi's. I'm constructing the phrasing in my head to put my guys in for Army Achievement Medals.

"You all right?" Sergeant King asks, standing next to me outside the passenger window. "Let me just get one more thing." He puts the Pepsi's in the trunk and goes back into his house. I notice he's wearing a jacket now. I jot a phrase in my notebook that I'll later use while writing up AAMs.

I start feeling hungry and more aware of the hot chicken grease smell in the car. I don't know how long Sergeant King is going to take but I know the chicken will be cold if I ever get a piece. I consider how unjust it is that "Ken Doll" will probably end up with the hottest chicken.

I won't learn until later what Sergeant King went back inside for. He had gone in the pantry for the Pepsi's when he heard his wife's mid-coitus groans coming from the bedroom. The ceiling fan rocking above the bed covered the sound of the opening door.

Two chains hang loose, gently swaying beneath the fan. The musky room suggests several hours of uninterrupted lovemaking. SSG King is already locked a loaded magazine into the well. We eventually learn he had more mags and ammo hiding in his garage.

He waits a moment before chambering the first round. His wife, Charlene, has her bare backside to the door as he enters. She's saddled on a neighbor named Ross who is a welder at the III Corps motor pool. I'll never learn Ross's rank or his last name.

When Sergeant King chambers a round, his wife is startled off of Ross the welder with a sudden pop. She yanks a condom off his steel girder with her Kegel action grip. The surprise triggers a physiological response causing Ross to arc spurts of hot DNA adhesive into several small puddles on the black satin bedspread.

SSG King jumps up onto the king sized bed, standing, looming over them with his rifle. His wife and the welder cower at the pillow end as the ceiling fan chains rest on the top of Sergeant King's head. They plead with him from their meek fetal positions.

I did not actually see any of this, mind you. As I said, I'm sitting in the front passenger seat of SSG King's car. I only hear the shot. I think about running inside but not for very long. I lean over to the driver's side and pop the trunk.

Only one of our rifles is there. Whisky Papa 3971497. It's my serial number. Thank god. I'm still going to jail but my weapon wasn't used for a murder. After a moment I don't hear any more shots. I figure what's happened so I close the trunk and get back in the car to wait for the MPs.

It turns out Sergeant King had pushed the M-16's barrel tightly into the underside of his Adam's apple then he splattered fragments of *corpus callosum* all over the blades of the ceiling fan.

I'm watching the single pair of MPs go inside and they don't come out for a while. I think about leaving the crime scene before I get too involved. I think about taking my rifle out of the trunk and pretending I was never here. Nobody saw me.

I don't have to, but I just patiently wait here to be arrested. Two wrongs don't make a right. I wonder about my guys. In case your curious, they all get fed eventually—even "Ken Doll"—thanks to the Mortar platoon having ordered plenty of pizza.

It takes nearly two minutes before the second pair of MPs park their cruiser behind where the first pair of MPs parked theirs. This is going to be a long night. I take a long controlled exhale, and then I breathe in a whiff of hot chicken grease. I reach behind my seat and produce a chicken leg, which is fortunately still very hot.

shackles

Adam Cloys

"Love is doing me good." That's what Leilani tells me. Not to sound cynical, but doesn't it always start out that way. It does not always end that way, but if it didn't start out like that would we even have love? We all know love totally sucks but if it started out like that it just wouldn't work at all. People would never be suckered into it in the first place. People would say: Oh you're in love, that sucks.

But that's not really the way it is, because it never hurts to be falling. It hurts to suddenly stop. That's my time in the military in a nutshell. You might say: Thirteen years in the Army, that sucks. Of course you would be right. It's bound to suck. It did suck, but it didn't always suck.

When you're just getting started you love it. 1997. Everything is new. Everything is novel; Basic training, AIT, first promotion, first duty station, first JRTC, first deployment, first time scoring expert with a rifle, first promotion board, first NCO school, first re-enlistment, and first PCS.

That was the honeymoon for me; that was my first two years. Totally falling in love with it. During that honeymoon I always had a smile on my face. Before I left Fort Drum my first OIC told me not to ever stop smiling. It was Jenny telling Forest not to ever stop running. My smile kept me going through the worst of what was yet to come.

Next thing I know, the honeymoon is over but I'm still married to it. Still married to my wife, still married to the Army. Second duty station. New unit as an NCO. Fort Hood. New responsibility. First NTC. Second deployment. Setting up Camp Virginia. First time having to be on someone's suicide watch. First Red Cross. Second promotion board. Redeployment to Fort Hood. Second NCO school. Orders for Korea. Four years in. Still smiling.

In Korea my smile was especially genuine. By then I wore a smile and a combat patch because I had deployed to Kuwait already. It seemed like a pretty good deal at the time. I would have plenty opportunity to earn my combat patch later. I had only deployed to Bosnia and Kuwait so I didn't really know the meaning of war. 2002. Instinctively I knew that this was as good as it was ever going to get and it wasn't going to get this good again.

I didn't know I was at the halfway mark of my career. I was about six years in.

Combat Support Coordination Team One intelligence section in support of the First ROK Army. Managing the Camp Long movie theater all volunteer staff on our off time. Second Red Cross Message. Tour cut short. My mother's funeral. Dark depression shadow creeping.

Signing back in to Fort Hood. Second JRTC. First time to war. Fourth overseas tour; Baghdad. Did you know they won't build a Walmart in Baghdad? There's a Target on every corner. First soldier to chapter out for pregnancy. First soldier to chapter out for drug addiction. Another promotion board. Another redeployment to Fort Hood. Third time having someone on suicide watch. Why the hell do people want to kill themselves so much?

Injury. Feeling overwhelmed with responsibility. Still smiling. Still depressed. Divorce from wife but not from Army. Promotion to senior ranks. Orders for next unit to Iraq. Second time at war; Military Transition Team in support of Iraqi Army in Baqubah. Second detainee facility. Getting shot at. Managing Local National Interpreters. Still smiling.

Loading wounded onto MEDEVAC helicopter. 2008. Threat of being taken hostage. Threat of death. Depression meds. Thyroid malfunction. Surgery. Thyroid meds. Back to finish Iraq tour.

Return, now years after honeymoon and I'm still smiling. Stop Loss. Third time to war whether I want to or not. Another unit.

Another NTC. Another JRTC. Some other so and so on suicide watch. Another deployment. Redundancy reigns. Giving up on being a lifer; I settle for being alive. Just to live through another War. Mosul, Iraq. Fear of death. Deepest depression. Full of sadness for humanity. Still smiling. It's good to be in love but mostly it really sucks.

That's just my love affair in summary. Those are the broad brushstrokes; I have to zoom way out to give a sense of the scope and I have to zoom way in to give the details. My story in detail takes decades to tell. It makes me want to write fiction instead. That would be fun. That could be exciting, gripping, concise. Not exciting like fiction. My anecdotes seem humdrum compared to battle scenes in war movies. But you don't want a story. You want my story.

There's the time in Baqubah, having to handcuff a detainee. Anyone cuffed or caged is a detainee. The Iraqi Army base here had a detainee facility. The 2/5 IA; the Second Brigade of the 5th Division of the Iraqi Army and I dealt with hundreds of caged men. I looked them in the eye.

Our MiTT consisted of about 25 Americans on a separate part of that Iraqi Army base. This was my overseas tour number five of six; my second time to go to war. I had been around caged men before but that wasn't even my job. At best it was one of my "hats." My official purpose was as a senior intelligence advisor for the Iraqi Brigade intelligence section. Sounds too easy, right?

These were my orders. This was my duty but simultaneously I was wearing other "hats," responsible for such things as detainees, interpreters, classified documents, and base camp security. It was part fun and part scary but mostly redundant. Somehow I was still smiling.

It should not have surprised me what happened when we learned that one of my interpreters could no longer be trusted; I had to cuff him.

Me? I wondered

Are you sure? I smiled

My Sergeant Major was absolutely sure I was the one to do it. We scheduled to have him picked up and I practiced with my handcuffs in private. I walked up to him and said some stuff I was supposed to say and I put cuffs on a man I had trusted. He had trusted me too.

There was no scuffle, no denying any wrongdoing, no resisting. It all went down in the most anticlimactic way possible. Other soldiers were around me with their loaded weapons drawn. The detainee wasn't going anywhere. I saw that familiar look in his eye that I had seen in other people's that were in his situation. No ending date assigned. Indefinite.

I wasn't smiling.

In the words of *System of a Down* singer Serj Tankian

> *There is no flag that is large enough*
> *To hide the shame of a man in cuffs*

There's no denying I'm part of that system now. Maybe I never pointed a weapon at anyone but I may have taken a man's life away just the same.

That's all you get from nonfiction sometimes. The story is often over before you ever see it coming. Immediately our lives moved on to the next thing. There was always more to do. But this wasn't the case for the man in cuffs. He was on his way to be a man in a cage and a man can sometimes be stuck in a cage for a long time.

Are you still there? I wonder

The Family Members

How do I tell this story? I have never experienced childbirth or even been pregnant. How can I possibly know what was in my mother's mind the day she gave birth to her first child, my brother in June of 1943. I was in my fifties when she first told me of her experience that day and I regret not pushing her for more details, answers to questions that I wish I had asked. She has been gone now over ten years, but I was so intrigued by her account that I decided to use what she told me as inspiration for the following short story as biographical fiction.

Firstborn

Dallas Dorsett Mathers

It's time, she thought. *The baby is coming.* Anna, a pretty, dark-haired twenty-three year old and her husband, Joe, a handsome young lieutenant in the United States Army, had talked about the possibility of it happening while he was at work. She knew what she was supposed to do. She was to call a cab and have it take her to Walter Reed Army Hospital, several miles away from their small home in a group of simple white wooden houses provided by the Army for families of servicemen. When she arrived at the hospital she was to check herself in and the staff would alert her doctor and call her husband.

Anna knew what to expect concerning childbirth. She grew up on a ranch in Oklahoma in the 20's and had seen enough animals give birth not to be shocked, or afraid of the things her body would soon go through; but she and her husband had made plans for the baby to be born with the doctor present so she wasted no time gathering the pre-packed bag and other things she needed for the hospital.

She went to the telephone and dialed the number for the taxi company. Anna wished she had been able to call her husband. He was working in what was called the Intelligence Unit at the nearby Aberdeen Proving Ground. What he was doing was top secret and he could be reached only through his superiors. She had a special phone number with instructions for informing Joe on a piece of

91

paper to give the doctor when she got to the hospital.

Joe's job both intrigued and frightened Anna. The United States was fighting in the Pacific against the Japanese and in North Africa against Hitler and Mussolini, and from what she had heard they would soon be fighting in Europe. Anna knew little of what was going on in the world. Her life was consumed with keeping house for her husband and preparing for the new baby. And, her knowledge of war and the reasons they were fought was limited to history lessons from school. She had been worried by recent newsreels of battles that showed explosions, fire, and soldiers running through smoke; and she knew both war theaters were taking heavy casualties. Joe tried to reassure her, but Anna was still afraid that his job might eventually take him into harm's way.

As Anna sat on the steps outside her little white house waiting for the taxi, a chill ran through her even though it was late June and the weather was luxuriously warm. What if something went wrong with the baby? She had been reassured by the doctor that everything was normal with her pregnancy however, so she willed the thought out of her mind, and instead, focused on getting to the hospital in time and according to plan. In a few minutes the yellow cab appeared around the curve of the road, slowed and stopped in front of Anna. The driver's eyes widened, seeing Anna's condition. The sandy-haired young man, wearing a gray shirt buttoned to the collar and a cap with the insignia of the Yellow Cab Company on the front, hopped out to help her into the cab along with her bag.

"I'm going to Walter Reed Hospital." Anna said, "Do you know how to get there?"

"Yes, Ma'am. It's in D.C., a pretty good ways from here, but I'll get you there as quick as I can," said the driver, and then the two barely spoke for the rest of the two-hour trip.

Anna settled down in the back seat of the cab and tried to get comfortable. Her water had broken a few hours earlier and she knew contractions would be starting soon. Leaning back against the seat, Anna thought of her mother, Myra, who was on her way by train and would get there tomorrow. Anna had hoped that Myra would arrive before the baby came, but saw now that she would be disappointed. At least it was comforting to know her mother would be there to help her with the newborn.

Anna watched the lush green landscape of Southern Maryland roll by outside the taxi's window and soon drifted off into a light sleep. She dozed for several minutes until the baby moved and she felt the first labor pain. Anna clenched her fists and tightened her jaw against the pain, but after only a few seconds it abated. She let out a small groan, startling the driver causing him to glance in the rear view mirror and slow the taxi. "I'm okay," she said, smiling, and he focused his attention back on his driving.

In spite of the pain, Anna felt reassured that things were going along as expected. She took a deep breath as she ran her hand over her swollen belly, feeling the warmth and the heartbeat of her baby and promising to do her best to take care of the little one soon to be born.

It was late afternoon when the taxi approached the imposing structure housing the Walter Reed Medical Center. The sprawling red brick building did not appear to have any clearly marked entrance or other sign pointing them in the right direction. The driver looked confused as he drove closer, following the street that wound around the building.

It was getting darker. The sun was setting, and the large trees surrounding the hospital were casting long shadows against the walkways making it harder to read what limited signage there was.

"Well, Ma'am, where would you like me to drop you? I'm not seeing a sign for the Admitting Office or anything," said the young driver, pulling the taxi to a stop next to the curb.

Anna looked out the window and noticed a small white sign near a walkway that said "Ward B" in black letters, and had an arrow pointing to a set of double doors at the end of one long wing of the huge building. The entrance was close so Anna told the driver she would go inside there. Relieved, the young man got out, helped Anna with her bag and walked beside her up the path. Finding the door unlocked, he pulled it open for her and set the bag inside.

"This okay, Ma'am?" said the driver, a little unsure. Anna smiled at him, reached in her purse, took out some money and paid him.

"Thanks. Yes, I'll be fine. I'm sure there is someone inside who will tell me where I'm supposed to go. Don't worry," she said. The driver hesitated a moment then turned to leave.

"Okay, then … uh, good luck, Ma'am," he called out over his shoulder as he sprinted back to his cab.

Ward B was a large room with abnormally high ceilings. *Almost like a cathedral,* Anna thought as she stepped inside. What light that was left in the day was filtering through the translucent shades covering large vertical windows, which were on opposite sides of the room. The windows were placed evenly, with military precision about five feet apart, giving the room the appearance of infinite depth.

Along the walls, placed perpendicular to them were rows of metal hospital beds, each containing a wounded soldier, neatly tucked in. It was strangely quiet and most of the men seemed to be either asleep or dosing. Beside each bed was a metal tray on a stand and a single straight-backed metal chair.

I must be careful not to disturb these men, Anna thought, although not one of the soldiers appeared to have even noticed her. She picked up her bag and took a few steps. The room seemed to go on forever—no exit in sight—no door other than the one from which she entered. She noticed that except for her own heart beating, the room had become deathly silent. Not even a breath could be heard.

Anna peered down the aisle between the rows of beds. *How many beds are there*? she wondered. *There are too many to count. Where have they all come from?* She paused momentarily then gathered herself and searched ahead for an exit to the hallway where surely she would find someone to help her.

Anna took several steps down the aisle then suddenly felt a sharp labor pain that was so strong it almost brought her to her knees. She set her bag on the floor and held on to it to keep from falling. *Don't cry out*, she willed herself, squeezing her eyes shut. *Don't wake the soldiers*. The pain subsided after several seconds. When she opened her eyes, she looked up hoping to see the exit to the hallway, but all she could see was a gray fog looming in the aisle a few feet in front of her.

Anna tried to tell herself that it must be her imagination, but she was afraid and her legs were trembling as she tried to walk a few more steps. She felt heavy and stiff. Soon she had to stop, fearing she would fall and hurt the baby. Her eyes filled with tears. She covered her face with her hands and struggled to suppress a sob. She had been so sure she was ready for what was happening to her, but now she wasn't.

As she stood there, frozen, she thought she felt someone coming from behind her. She looked up and a figure brushed past her right shoulder. It was a tall man in an old-fashioned military uniform, a blue coat, black tri-cornered hat, and he was carrying a sword which he thrust at the fog in front of Anna, then disappeared into it, all in an instant. "Wait," Anna called after him, but the figure had come and gone so quickly, she knew it must have been her eyes playing tricks on her. Besides, she reasoned, she had not actually seen the man, had she? It was more like she had felt his presence, like in a dream or a memory.

The fog in front of her seemed to have lightened, so Anna rubbed her eyes and forced herself to move a few more feet down the aisle. Then the fog emitted a swishing sound and sent long dark tendrils toward her, stopping her in her tracks. She stood not moving. The tendrils circled around Anna. "Please, don't hurt us," Anna implored. This time she felt something move by her on the left. It was another soldier, from another time. He had a black beard and was wearing what Anna thought was the blue uniform of a Union officer. He was carrying a rifle, bayonet attached. *This isn't real*, Anna told herself as the soldier silently drove back the tendrils with his bayonet and vanished, taking the fog with him, in a heartbeat.

I'm just dreaming, Anna thought. *I must keep moving.* She looked ahead into the fog and saw light coming from the center. *That must be the exit!* she decided, strengthening her resolve. As she stepped forward her body was suddenly wrenched by another excruciating labor pain. Tears came and she doubled over, almost collapsing to the floor. She lifted her head to call out but was only able to moan. Then she saw a tall, lean young man dressed in a strange green military uniform she had never seen before. At first she thought it was Joe. On the young man's jacket, a name she couldn't quite make out was embroidered over one pocket and "U.S. Army" over the other. The young man was smiling. *He has the cutest dimples*, she thought, oddly. He held out his hand to Anna and, as she took it, the pain subsided and suddenly she felt she was going to be okay. Then she fainted.

A few moments later she awakened. She was lying on a stretcher and a nurse in a starched white uniform and cap was holding her hand.

"There you are! Hello. What's your name, Dear?" she asked in a heavy southern drawl.

"Anna. I'm supposed to see Dr. Ryan," she answered, looking around for her purse. "I have some papers and the phone number."

Finding her purse next to her on the stretcher, she retrieved the information and handed it to the nurse. The nurse glanced at the paper and called over a couple of burly orderlies in white uniforms.

"Take her over to Hallway 17," the nurse told them, then turned to Anna. "It's our temporary maternity unit, Dear. I'll call ahead and Dr. Ryan will meet you there."

The orderlies easily lifted Anna and carried her down the hall, through what seemed like an endless maze of doorways and corridors and finally lifted her into a bed in an open room where there were other women awaiting childbirth. Relieved to be where she was supposed to be, Anna closed her eyes and breathed deeply, taking advantage of the few moments of calm before the start of the next labor pains.

Her doctor soon appeared, looked Anna over, pronounced everything proceeding normally and disappeared, leaving her in the care of the nurses who would summon him when the baby was ready to be born.

Anna's mind wandered between labor pains, but she wouldn't let herself dwell on the visions from the fog. She was told that her husband had arrived at the hospital and was in the waiting room just outside the maternity ward. He would be able to come to her as soon as the baby was born, so she wanted to do as much as she could to make that happen quickly.

It seemed like forever to Anna, but finally the Doctor arrived to deliver the baby. The nurses pulled a screen around her bed for privacy. Then the doctor, sitting on a stool between her legs, told her to push and one of the nurses held her hand. After one last mighty effort, Anna felt the tiny body slip out of her womb. She opened her eyes to see the doctor holding the baby, freshly born and covered in fluids.

"It's a boy!" announced the doctor and the infant let out a loud cry. The doctor cut the umbilical cord and handed the baby to a nurse who cleaned him, then wrapped a blanket around him and handed him to Anna.

Anna had never felt so much love for anything before and could not take her eyes off the new young life she held in her arms. Then she heard Joe's voice.

"Anna?"

She looked up to see her husband, his hair a mess, tie undone and uniform wrinkled, but still the most handsome man she had ever seen.

"Are you all right?" he said staring at her, eyes wide.

"It's a boy, Joe. And, look! He's got the cutest dimples."

Anna pulled the blanket away from the baby's face and showed him to Joe who sat gently on the bed taking mother and son in his arms.

When I Was Waiting To Be Born

Mary Lu Coughlin

A line from a poem "When I was waiting to be born" opened the portal to my memories and this writing. I decided to attend Leilani's class (Writing Your Story: An Exploration of Your Life in the Military) because I have been actively involved with veterans at Wellness Works as well as having two brothers, a nephew and a great nephew who are veterans. I wanted to find what this meant to me.

Listening to the public readings of the veterans writing group is profoundly touching. I have come to believe that this work of writing one's story, one's truth, is a fundamental source of healing and wholeness. For veterans to write about war and their military life from personal experience and to be able to read those words aloud and to be listened to by others takes an act of courage and strength. This willingness to bear the veterans' suffering restores a sense of soul to the wounded soldier, the family member, and the listener.

Leilani brought a poem to the first class, "The Portrait" by Stanley Kunitz. After reading it aloud, she asked what line spoke to us. For me, the line midway through his poem, *when I was waiting to be born* was it. The image captured my imagination. With our line selected, we were instructed to write for 20 minutes not letting our pencils stop. Just keep going. And so I did.

My first day's writing revealed my mother's version of that time. June 1941 through March 1942 marked the time when I was waiting to be born. Pearl Harbor is the pop up here. And the fact our family lived in Los Angeles at the edge of the Pacific Ocean, the reality of war and danger was present. As it happened, there was a black out that night, March 22nd, and my mother could not get to the hospital as planned. Instead she was brought to St. Anne's Home for Unwed Mothers, a charity for pregnant young girls closer to our home. She was 38 at this time and was not prepared for that level of humiliation as she felt it to be. There she was in a four-bed ward with three young teenage girls preparing to give birth to babies who were to be adopted. As my mother told this story over many years, somehow always her shame and my blame were felt together.

After that first class, the picture of the night when I was waiting to be born lingered within me. My first writing helped me touch into fears my mother never named. Fears of the darkness, of arriving at this unfamiliar place, being placed with girls half her age, giving birth to a third child, her first daughter in the midst of the world's uncertainty, and the uncertainty of her immediate future as well. My father who was 32 had been alerted months earlier of his potential draft status. Both my parents had to have wondered how they would manage with their budding young family of three children, six, four and me their newborn.

War and its fears dominated this first story and awakened my curiosity. How were my earliest years influenced by World War II? How did nations—East and West—fighting in the belief that might makes right impact me? It is clear that not only while I was waiting to be born but from my first night, war and its fears and uncertainties tried to define my sense of being here, being human.

My two brothers were six and four and played war every day. A childhood photo shows Jay, my oldest brother, helmet on, rifle strapped across his shoulder, peddling his tricycle, red wagons loosely connected into a makeshift train trailing behind him, leading the neighborhood platoon down the sidewalk, parade fashion. And there, at the end of the train on the last wagon, a little chair facing backwards, sits me, the baby, propped up, staring backwards at the trail behind us.

While they were away at school, many days I played imaginary games outdoors by myself. When I was almost four, I remember being in the back yard with a big kitchen tablespoon in hand, on my knees, digging giant spoonfuls of dirt from under the lone tree. My brothers had overheard adults talking about America needing to get to China so Jay and Jerry made a plan to dig a hole to get there. I distinctly remember feeling important working with this dirt, each spoonful adding to the mountain by my side and the hole getting bigger and deeper. I was helping to end the war.

I love two pictures in my baby book. Both of them show me dressed like my mother's little girl. But in both photos, if you look closely, you see one of my brother's toy-German Lugars sticking out of my skirt waist, there on the right side.

But along with playing war, there were the newsreels. Sitting in a darkened theatre, each week people viewed current newsreels, stark black and white film, fast moving images of bombing and death, sounds of air raid whistles screaming, destruction of cities, people, refugees staring into the camera, hospitals filled with the wounded and maimed, children orphaned, soup lines and food shortages, troops marching through jungles with terror accompanying every step, and worst of all, the visions of living skeletons standing behind barbed wire fences at places called concentration camps.

With each writing class, I remembered more vividly my early experiences. My personal timeline of history became real for me. I began to feel the stories of my life in a new way and could see how they formed my earliest childhood ideas of war, solving conflicts and of knowing right and wrong.

And so it was that war and its myth penetrated my sense of being human. By the time I was five, nothing I heard or experienced influenced me to think differently. For in fact, this myth played itself out in our family life, in the way my father physically disciplined my brothers when my mother complained of their fighting with each other. And in turn, my older brother over time learned how to bully his younger brother. Gradually, might makes right moved in and lived in our house, fear and anger took their place at our table.

It was in first grade that hope arrived. It came in the form of Sister Mary Vivian and my first religion classes. When she asked the catechism question, who made me, and the answer revealed God made me. I was shocked. And then the second question, why did God make me? And the answer: to know, love and serve God and be happy with God forever. My heart grabbed at these words. I knew in an instant they were true. I knew the reason that I was born. I knew why I was here.

How sweet and wise the child's heart.

At this point, I stopped writing what I was writing. I had gotten myself in a dither. Too much thinking.

The following poem got me unstuck and concludes for now, what happened when I was waiting to be born.

When I was waiting to be born, I raised my little spirit hand
YES. YES. YES.

Let me go, let me go. I want to go to earth. I want to go.
I want to learn to be a body and soul. All together.
Yes, yes, I want to go.

But whoa, the very first night, this was not what I expected.
Way different.

It was like somebody, help.

Hey, where is everybody?

That's how I see it now.
Life is a moment to moment shock.

Breathing is a gift to help us take it in, let it out
and have a pause before we start all over again.

Yes, this is what it has taken me 75 years to learn
about being all together. Body and soul.

Moment to moment.

Don't get caught in thinking.

I did.

It's horrible. Horrible.
It has taken me 75 years and some days more
to figure this out.
Sadie my dog, she's a Yellow Lab. Eight years old.
She is my guru on this.
Sadie is on the floor here. Her stuffed dog Ralph in her mouth.
Waiting for me to take her out and play.

I will write more later.
Stay tuned.
But first things first.

Oh yeah, after working (for Labs play and work overlap)
Sadie always comes in and sleeps awhile.
Likewise for me.

This activity of being born moment to moment
looks better every breath cycle.

But trust me, it takes a lot of notches on your timeline
to get this.

Just keep practicing.

Reading and Books and the Military Family

Sandra Squire Fluck

My passion for books began in my childhood. I remember like it was yesterday, savoring the book I was reading as we drove across the United States on our way from the East Coast to the West Coast, where my father would be stationed next. We were a military family and we went where my father, a Chief Petty Officer in the Navy, had received new orders. These orders were always on the coast—east or west—along with a stint in Hawaii before it was a state.

We moved often during my childhood, our residences Quonset huts, apartments, duplexes—one time a so-called house resembling a hut—for a year, two or three months, a few weeks, or sometimes a couple of days. When we returned to the states from Hawaii, our living quarters weren't available, so we camped out for two weeks in Yosemite National Park. When I was eleven years old, my father was transferred to Coronado Naval Air Station, San Diego, and my parents bought our first home. I didn't realize stability meant something other than packing up and moving and leaving friends—none of whose names I remember to this day. By the time I was twelve years old, I had attended sixteen different schools.

My education as a child didn't happen only in the classroom. I have my father and mother to thank for that. My father drilled me on my arithmetic tables, the roll call of states and their capitals, and important historical dates and events, and he enlivened my imagination with colorful stories about the places he had visited around the world. Then there was this beautiful land of ours. My sisters and I watched captivated, as we traveled across the plains, through the desert, and into the mountains. It must have been during these trips when I fell in love with the desert, sensing that I had found a peace in the austerity of the heat. We bought our food supplies in grocery stores or at stands along the way, and ate our lunches and dinners in parks and on the side of the road. As I remember it, we never once ate in a restaurant or stayed overnight in a motel.

Books took me away from myself, sparked my imagination, and nourished my mind and soul. Even with the back-and-forth between my father and me, the stories he told, and the games my mother and sisters and I invented to try to trick each other, I still needed books. My mother took care of this for me. She was adamant about giving us the best education she could, even as our classroom experience was transient. You could say the books she bought saved me during these trips—and beyond. Although I didn't know it then, books were my escape from the instability in my life—moving from place to place often and enrolling in schools for maybe just a day or week. I was an introverted, shy girl, and it couldn't have been easy making friends with the other children when I didn't know how long they and I would be together. I thought my life was normal, that other families moved around as we did, but it didn't seem to matter then. I had my books, a circumstance precisely made for me.

I immersed myself in books, read them as if they were my best friends, poured my heart into them. Sometimes at night when my father or mother had pulled over to the side of the road to sleep, I took out my trusty flashlight to read the last pages of my novel in the dark that surrounded us. Books took me away from myself, sparked my imagination, and nourished my mind and soul.

He was angry about something

Justine Helena Bugaj

He was angry about something
What it was
I do not remember
But his anger needed no reason

Just as his hate needed forgiveness
Just as his hurt needed solace
      on those Sunday morning visits
      to the assembled masses
      of prayer and short-lived absolution

I grieved with him on days
Wondering what haunted him so
Questioning if there was any peace he could find
In his steps through the door
To a day-to-day life

He was angry about something
What it was
I do not remember
But his wrath needed no reason

He barreled through the kitchen
In search of an enemy
Finding only me
What had I done? Who had I become?
It no longer mattered what reality existed
The corner was turned, the switch ignited

Sensing this rage moving on its own

without caution or rationale,
I ran
The locked bedroom door, my 10-foot concrete wall
The thundering footsteps seeking my name

I am no longer here.
My head buried in the covers
I dream of other places
Fear, my forever friend, sits at the edge of the bed

Footsteps halt
Uncensored murmurs of confusion slip under the door
Disoriented silence
The footsteps part ways
Seeking other refuge, in a different foxhole

My wall sufficed, this time
I remember to breathe
But the things he carried
home from the war
Have been dropped at my door too.

Sharing his burden of seen unseen
Without speaking
Without knowing
Without wanting

Apricot Jam

Justine Helena Bugaj

Those trees in the backyard
Promised happiness
Sustenance
Reminders of brilliant warmth
Captured by a single fruit

Reaching to pick nature's effort
Harvesting memories the tree holds
I harken to a time when one melts into another

Presiding in her kitchen, holding trade to the art of food
Making sweet treat to remember her by
To share her past with a present moment
That lives now in a reflecting dream

I still taste it
I still see her standing over heat
Stirring rhythmically while her lean body and tower of hair
Melt the juices
Coalescing the paste of sweetness
For our enjoyment

It was, in its essence, a selfless act
A gift to her grandchildren
That memory
That apricot jam

Midnight Watch

Leilani Squire

My father served thirty years in the Navy during three wars. He was deployed many times on aircraft carriers and other ships that crossed the seas to Okinawa, Japan, and other lands. He catapulted planes and jets and thrived on the excitement and danger of the flight deck. He was also a mechanic who worked on the jets and proud and good at his job. But he also liked the solitude of standing watch onboard these ships, perched here and there, waiting and listening for a sign of something, or nothing. Growing up, I was used to him being absent for months and then coming home for a few months, and then leaving again. I was sad when he left and happy when he came home. It may seem odd to civilians, but it's the way it is for a military family.

After he retired from the Navy in 1964, he hung around the house piddling the days away with small tasks in the garage and the backyard. With a few years of retirement under his belt, he became bored and decided he wanted to drive a taxi. So he became an employee of the Yellow Cab Co. and worked the late shift. My father loved driving all over San Diego and meeting the different kinds of people who hailed his taxi. He enjoyed talking to his customers and listening to their stories, he told me. And then he would tell me his stories about them.

In 1974, when I was twenty-three, married and living in an apartment on the beach, I woke up one day with severe pain in my abdomen. I felt like I was dying, and I was taken to the emergency room in the town I grew up in and admitted to the hospital. Within hours, Dr. Miller, the resident surgeon/gynecologist, performed exploratory surgery to find out what the problem was. The intrauterine device that had been inserted into my vagina three years before had perforated my uterus. He removed a cyst the size of an orange in my right ovary and a cyst the size of a grapefruit in my uterus. He also removed my right ovary and right fallopian tube because they were too damaged to keep. Dr. Miller couldn't find the IUD and so he sewed me back up. Soon after the surgery, I was placed in isolation for ten days, or maybe two weeks. It could have been three weeks. I don't remember. A lot of things are mixed up in my memory, and yet other things are crystal clear, and I remember them as if they happened an hour ago. Like Dr. Miller standing by the bed in the room in the farthest corner of the ward, looking down at me and saying, "You have a rare infection." I never learned the name of the infection, or if it even had a name. Maybe he didn't know what was complicating and hindering my recovery—the rarity that was eating away the tiny cilia inside the remaining fallopian tube. At another time, he told me I was being given Vitamin K intravenously for my blood. Maybe my blood needed a boost after the blood transfusion. Maybe the infection was doing something to my blood. I don't know. "It's expensive," he said. But I didn't care. I didn't have health insurance, but I didn't care about that either.

I do remember—and always will—the haunting silence within the corridors of the night when my father came to the hospital after he finished his shift at the Yellow Cab Co. to don the regulation robe and shoe coverings and mask the nurse handed him. He entered the isolation room and carefully greeted the fragments my life had become. It looked like I lay in the bed watching and waiting or sleeping, but he knew I was moving through another universe— slipping into the vast and silent place where the will to live balances between here and that other place.

Sometimes I would wake up around midnight and wait for the sound of my father's voice as he greeted the night nurse. She reported to him my condition. Their voices lowered then so I couldn't hear what they said. They didn't want me to know what I already knew: Something terribly wrong was happening to me and no one could stop it and no one really knew what would or could happen. I was in uncharted territory. We all were. The medical technology wasn't what it is today. I often wonder what would happen if the IUD perforated my uterus today. But it couldn't happen now because the intrauterine devices that were inserted into women in the early 1970s were taken off the market after too many of them perforated uteruses and too many women died from the damage done by the not-tested-enough-and-put-on-the-market-too-soon contraceptive device. In a way, those early IUDs did their jobs stopping pregnancies. They killed women. They maimed the reproductive organs of the ones who lived so badly that they were unable to bare children. I'm one of those women. In a way, I'm one of the lucky ones to have had the Loopis Loop, instead of the deadly Dalcon Shield.

When I was awake, I watched my father walk through the door and hesitate to see if I were awake or asleep—to check if his youngest daughter was really inside this room of isolation. I listened to the rustle of the blue cloth gown, the muted sound of his footsteps with the slippers covering his shoes. His voice sounded muffled behind the mask as he said hello. He pushed a chair to the farthest corner away from me and read articles from his right-winged health journal while I lay in the hospital bed. I still see him sitting there, so quietly, so focused. I see the four-page newsletter, the brown color of ink, the title scrawling across the top of the front page. His weathered well-traveled traveling bag tucked between the chair and the wall. The absence of a window to gaze outside, to see where the moon was, know which stars had risen, which ones were setting. I watched my father as he read to me. He wanted me to know about the benefits of juicing, raw food, balance and exercise. I listened to his voice, not the content of the articles because I didn't care about balance. What does balance mean to a young woman too weak to watch television? How would a raw diet help me now? I can't walk to the nurses' station, how can I shop for organic spinach and parsley? I wondered.

But those questions or answers didn't really matter to me. It was the love I listened to, it was my father's voice, his gentle reckoning of his daughter that I let seep into me, and ease a part of me. Could it be that he knew it was his chance to make up for all the nights he didn't read to his little girl because he was away serving his country on board ship somewhere far away? Was he reaching back to the time when I was a child and missing my Daddy and he missed me, and somehow those nights inside the hospital were his chance to be redeemed for being absent so many days and nights?

Sometimes I woke up and he would be sitting in the chair he had pushed into the corner farthest away from my bed. He would be sitting there, quietly, watching, waiting for me to waken. And then he would smile and that smile was like a star inside the starless night shining only for me. My father standing watch in the corner of that room saved me. His presence was my medicine. His showing up every night, at almost the same moment, to watch over his youngest daughter was my lifeline.

What did he think, sitting in the corner, in the middle of the tomb-like night of the hospital? I don't think I ever asked him. I don't think he ever told me. But I don't need to know now. His actions speak to me of a father's love, of a man who knew that this was the most important watch of his life.

I didn't leave that room for days. I don't remember how long I was in isolation. I can't remember because I was living in another realm, fighting for my life but it didn't seem like that to me. I was too weak, too sick to understand but still I knew. I could see it on the faces of my ballet teacher and another student who was my friend when they visited me. I could hear the trepidation in their voices, and see how they stood in the middle of the room away from the bed, covered in the regulation uniform, afraid to touch me. I saw on their faces the fear that they could end up like me. My mother and oldest sister's smiles and kind words couldn't hide the helplessness they felt, the fear that maybe I would die, as they stood by my beside, not knowing what to do. Maybe my veteran and ex-Underwater Demolition Team husband came to my bedside. I try to remember seeing him, but there's nothing there.

But my father? Never did I see helplessness or hopelessness or fear appear on his face. Never once did I hear in his voice anything but love and the determination that I would survive. He knew what he needed to do for his baby girl. What made my father defy the doctor's orders and lean over the railing of the hospital bed, and kiss my cheek, and stroke my forehead as he said a gentle goodnight? Was he born with this wisdom? Did he learn something in the Navy that enabled him to choose so wisely? Did he experience something during war that taught him how to act around the wounded?

That room in the middle of the night was our sanctuary. It was as if we were alone inside a place far removed from everyone and everything. It was like a catacomb the gods forgot to enter or didn't know existed, but I didn't need any gods. I had my father. He is the one who appeared at the door and entered the sad and lonely place where I lay in the hospital bed that was pushed against the wall, as far away from the door as possible but within reach of a nurse or doctor.

My father appeared when I needed him most and tossed a lifeline to me, knowing there was the possibility that I might not catch it. But that didn't stop him; he kept on appearing and throwing it to me. It was his appearance, his love, his concern, and his standing watch night after night that held me above the water I was drowning inside. It was the timbre of his voice that I grabbed on to, and held on to, inside the deepest corner of a diminishing will.

Events are all mixed-up. What happened before could have happened after. It's all a jumble, mish-mashed into a dream-like memory. Trauma does this to our psyches. Maybe the logical slips through the tear in our souls, leaving us confused about the whens, the whos, the whys. But this I do remember:

I waited, and listened for the soft-spoken nurse to greet my father. I listened for the arrival of his footsteps in the solemn hallway outside the isolation room. I listened as he approached this room cut off from the rest of the world where he brought his world to me.

What I carry....

Lisa Raggio

A lead-based portrait on parchment colored paper of a robust face looking head on, hat finely placed and medals on a khaki colored vest

I walked by this portrait every day for most of my youth

Invisibly saluting a man I've known since I could understand my mom's words but never met

Her adoration lives and breathes in her tones and the pauses she uses when reminiscing

His departure to the war at her formidable age

Left with her mother's growing reliance on the bottle to endure his absence

My mother's longing for his return when my grandmother became captor of ugliness and vile due to the bottle — four long years

Then the room — photos, memorabilia, their soul's ether flood the bedroom next to mine — of service, from my grandfather to brother,

deployments, flags, medals

A mother now of a son, pride in his promotions, worry, concern and fear with long absences and no word from my

brother,
A mom weeping in a bathroom and murmuring that she can't lose another son

My uncle, her brother, his tainted breath always, his disease, his children, all addicted to pills, alcohol, drugs- his service, his loss of marriage, children, life, cirrhosis, like his daughter, my cousin, on the other side, her end too early- life marked by tragedy

My uncle, her brother in law, marine, sharp, tough, witty, street smart, gone, his children, estranged, my cousin- dead, suicide, 6 kids left- 2 that speak to him

My brother- her son, my kindred spirit, letters in a box, just to me, of where he's been, what he's seen, soldier, first, soldier always

Brother's picture, grandfather's picture- same eyes, head, hair, mouth, stare — always up — toward the flag

Awakening to the planes, towers, fire, slow motion, my children asking me to go to school, the phone call, my sister in law, her service — Where is Paul? Where is Paul? Where is Paul? Can't find Paul....

A pentagon is on my TV. A child on each side of me. No school today. They can't find Paul.

Panoramic view of all above, over and over, grandfather's portrait, salute, my grandmother dying in drug recovery from alcohol withdrawals, my uncle's loss of wives and children, my mother's loss of father, brother, mother- how do I tell her- her son now gone and dead. Can't do it. Must do it. Need to prepare.

Scream at my babies- need silence. Need to hear all the words from the TV. Be a warrior. Be strong. Be responsible. Be dutiful. Like him. Like them.

Phone rings. His wife- my sis in law. He's found.

No. More. Loss. For. Me. My. Mother.

Crossroads

an op-ed

Glenn Schiffman

This country is at a crossroads. People, we have to choose: do we forge ahead for the common good or turn and go back to support the goods of selected individuals? Do we turn hard left to belong with those who deem human rights should prevail over property rights, or do we turn hard right to belong with those who think property rights trump human rights? That's the divide; those are the two camps. Commoners are the majority; a selected few have most of the property and money, which means they have the military and the police on their side.

The divide is not gender specific. It is gender evident. Women are leading the organized human rights demonstrations, and the resistance is greater numbers than ever before.

In 2007 my friend, fellow writer James Mathers, who was both a Navy and Air Force veteran, wrote a one page essay that began: *There's some movement. I smell change. I'm in my 70's so I remember change. You young ones out there don't recognize change because you've never seen it. So lemme tell you what it looks like. But before I do that you have to know what's going on right now. We got constant warfare on every continent on this planet, and we got a police state here at home.*

Why did he believe we have a police state here at home? Simply put, in all cases the way the laws are written, property rights trump human rights.

Now, it's important I explain the distinction between "human" rights and "civil" rights. The right to vote is a civil right. The right to protest is a civil right. Free speech is a civil right. When they are violated, we might get angry, but we most likely will survive. Human rights are undeniable necessities, which means they are about survival. Clean water is life, health care is life, education clears the way to having a life.

To quote James Mathers: *People run to Congress or the President and say, What the fuck, what's going on, education is our right, clean water is our right, health care is not a privilege but a right,* and the Speaker/Leader/President say, "No, it's all property. You want clean water, you have to buy it from Coke or Pepsi or Nestlé. You want health care, you have to pay for patented, overpriced pharmaceuticals and insurance premiums that provide minimal coverage but exorbitant executive salaries. Education? Sure, we'll give you public education, but just let us take 30% of those public dollars and fund private and charter schools for a few selected privileged kids." Oh, does that mean inner city schools pass kids through eight grades of bare-bones literacy? Sorry. Education is a privilege, not a human right.

Yes, *there is movement.* Millions of Americans now want the thugs out of Congress and out of the White House in order to prevent condemning the next generation of Americans to stupidity, unhealthiness, and mind-numbing labor jobs with no desperately needed bootstraps and no productive future.

As I write this, it's Spring 2017. That means there are young men and women graduating high school who were born in the year 2000. There are college graduates born in 1995, whose first possible memory of a presidential election is the one decided by one vote in the Supreme Court.

In 1992, 1600 leading scientists, including more than 100 Nobel laureates, signed a statement regarding the climate-change, global-warming crisis that concluded: "We, the undersigned, senior members of the world's scientific community, hereby warn all humanity: No more than <u>one or two decades</u> remain before the chance to avert the threats we now confront will be lost and the prospects for humanity immeasurably diminish."

There are graduate students getting Masters and Doctorates in science this year who were born in 1992, the year that warning was given.

Or, let me take you back 60 years. In 1957, two University of Illinois professors studying the population explosion and working with the proportional rate of increases of the previous century predicted that the suffocation point for human society from both pollution and over-population would come in the year 2025.

So, yes, *there is movement*, but it needs to grow into mass resistance, into rage against the machinery of the consolidators of property, or we are all going to suffocate. This year's graduates, be they 17, 22, or 27 need to lead. Artists, musicians, writers, poets, teachers, preachers, elders and wise, non-warmongering politicians must stand up and point the way.

I was a conscientious objector during the Vietnam War. I was also a graduate student in San Francisco, a member of SDS, and I was involved in many anti-war demonstrations, plus the People's Park demonstration, which was all about property, and as a graduate English teacher, I was personally involved with the San Francisco State College Strike.

Due to a "bargain" with my draft board, my resistance activities did not cost me my C.O. status, but it did cost me an open FBI file, which put me on the U.S. government's blacklist, which prevents me from ever being hired for any public school teaching jobs.

So I know something about demonstrating and about resisting, and if demonstrations and resistance are going to save human rights and lives in this country, I am willing to stand and tell you what I know:

First, every demonstration in this country today, even purportedly for a human right such as clean water, health care, or education, is actually a demonstration against property-right laws of owners, corporate boards, and banks. Even a woman's right to choose is a religious property issue; our government is protecting a religious rule stemming from the time when women were property.

Second, violent resistance doesn't work, not in a police state, because the police are always on the side of the owners, corporate, and banks. There's an old Russian saying: "If you want to get rich, make friends with the police."

The first time I was engaged in a bloody, riotous demonstration against the war was in 1967 in Oakland. Foremost in my memory are the moments of mob fury and police assaults followed by people backing up, regrouping and calm voices calling out, "Is everyone OK? Does anyone need help?" And then the chanting would start again; the roar and the fury would start again, and my survival mind would engage to avoid police batons giving me a beating.

I'll never forget the aroma of skull blood dripping into and combining with vinegar-soaked bandannas. I can still smell that over the air smoked with tire fires and tear gas.

I cannot fictionalize the reality of those demonstrations. In my mind's eye I see women and elders holding signs; their chanted slogans bouncing off storefronts, while young men curse and hurl stones and trash, then turn and run down alleys and side streets, only to be pushed back into police lines by rednecks and Hells Angels swinging axe handles.

I remember almost none of the chaotic storylines every one of those demonstrations tried to tell, because in truth the police in full battle array plowing their swat-armored trucks down the avenue narrated the main storyline. Children and old women tilled to the gutters by the swat trucks held up their peace signs in surrendering self-defense, only to watch the armored and shielded police sweep by, ignoring them, intent only on clubbing longhairs like me.

My one personal unwavering element in each demonstration was that I would always need to take a long piss just before the action started. When the first changes began to swell, and just as the police bullhorns were raised to warn that we were illegal and subject to arrest, my bladder would call. Before the hurling of bottles, the tying on of bandannas, and before the burning tear gas, I would take a long adrenaline-fired piss against some dumpster or light pole. I wasn't alone. I wasn't pissing out of fear. I don't know about the others, but like an animal, I was marking territory. I was telling the police that I was defending our land.

Now I'm in my mid-seventies, regarded by many as an old man, and I don't demonstrate, only because I can't run as fast as in those heady days in the 60's. But I can give advice. And my advice is: be non-violent, and be strategic about it, including sometimes working within the system, for instance, to find the way to overturn Citizens United. Don't destroy property; right or wrong, it will get your head bashed in.

Third, therefore, is be clear about "Why?" you are resisting. There are two kinds of anger: revenge and righteous anger. Regarding revenge, there's a Taoist saying: "If you seek revenge, dig two graves." Revenge is a hot coal you pick up to throw at someone else. It only burns you. Exacting revenge is not a viable reason to resist, whereas righteous anger is exactly that, RIGHTEOUS! But know that righteous anger requires both clarity and passion.

We must be clear in our minds about right and wrong and we must have a passion for the cause that comes from our hearts, not someone else's mouth. Understand that truth is a trunk with two branches. One branch is what's logical; the other is what's cultural. The trunk is what's accurate. Chairman Mao once said, "Political power comes from the barrel of a gun." That's logical. Napoleon once said, "God is on the side of the best artillery." That's cultural.

Neither one is accurate. These words of the Buddha have helped me identify what is accurate truth: "Believe nothing, no matter where you read it, or who said it, no matter if I have said it, unless it agrees with your own reason and your own common sense."

Fourth, know "where" we are collectively going. Know the long game, sequences, subsequences and consequences. Knowing "where" is about purpose, and in that purpose is the gravitas, the seriousness, the momentousness of the movement. More important-ly, knowing where we are going sustains faith.

"Blessed are those who hunger and thirst for righteousness, for they will be filled." Our goal, a place of righteousness, is Beatitude; a strategy through which we "seek to be in possession of all things held to be good."

The opposite of "beatitude" is "misery." Misery according to the Book of Luke, will come to "....those who are rich, for they have already received their comfort; those who are well fed now, for they will go hungry; they who laugh now, for they will mourn and weep; and to those of whom everyone falsely flatters, for that is how their ancestors treated the false prophets."

In order to inherit the Earth, we must trust that the strategies we need to succeed are found in the accurate history books, the old, oral stories handed down through the generations, and in the lessons and non-violent advice of those who have "been there, done that" in the 60's. Yes, we succeeded in bringing down Johnson and Nixon and we helped end a war, and we engendered enforceable clean water, voting rights, and civil rights laws. But we did it with tactics. We didn't have a coordinated strategy. Tactics are short-lived. People today must draw from the embers, not from the ashes of the past.

I have adapted some "Modern Beatitudes" as a basic strategy: (a) Successful are those who remain non-violent even while enduring evils inflicted on them by others. (Both MLK and Malcolm X were brilliant orators, but it was King whose hand is on the Civil Rights Act.) (b) Successful are those who pick up the causes of the abandoned and marginalized and show them true (not logical, not cultural) friendship. (Don't co-opt another culture for our political gain.) (c) Successful are those who protect and care for our common home, Mother Earth. (Nuf said.) (d) Successful are those who surrender their own comfort in order to help others. (Do not be a usurer.)

Fifth, efforts to save our environmental, health, and education human rights may very well start in our home communities. We will ask our home communities to open their eyes. Our neighbors will follow us if, unlike the majority of our current political leaders, we live and act with integrity. Integrity is the only thing in the universe that is motionless. We shouldn't act until we have found integrity within ourselves. Integrity is protection against being co-opted, being pressured and/or being "bought off." Here is an apocryphal story from Buddhist literature to demonstrate integrity:

"Do you know who I am?" said the officer to the monk after the monk refused to allow a Red Chinese battalion to quarter in a monastery. "I am one who could cut your head off with one swing of an ax, and I would never blink an eye."

"Do you know who I am?" said the monk. "I am one who could have his head cut off with one swing of an ax, and I would never blink an eye."

Integrity is eminently recognizable, and is beyond any perceptive definitions. I believe that the moment the monk found it within himself to face down the soldier, the soldier backed down. But, I'm also not preaching "carpe diem, seize the day." It does no good to dive for pearls in an ocean that doesn't have any.

The country is at a crossroads, so resistance to the reactionaries will take both integrity and audacity. During World War II, a young Quaker who applied for Conscientious Objector status appeared before his draft review board. After the Quaker made his case, the head officer, a reserve colonel, fumed:

"Where do you think you would be if you were in Nazi Germany?"

"I'd be dead or in a concentration camp," the young Quaker answered, and then he asked, "And you, Colonel Sir, where would you be if you were in Nazi Germany?"

The time has come to be that audacious.

This country is at a crossroads. James Mathers ended his essay with the plea, *If we've got any poets out there, the time has come to step up.* To that I add, if there are any elders out there, the time has come to be heard … again.

THE CONTRIBUTORS

Justine Helena Bugaj is a web designer, poet and published author of *Alex Moves to a New House*, a charming tale for young children. She is co-founder of the online websites bookscover2cover and thewritelaunch. She lives on the Cape with her husband, cats and roses. She enjoys a good book and a good podcast, running and swimming. Both of her grandfathers served in the U.S. military; one of her grandfathers was a BAR gunner and fought in the Battle of the Bulge and Remagen Bridge Head, and the other served in the Navy for thirty years during three wars.

Adam Cloys, SFC, was an intelligence analyst in the United States Army from 1997-2010. He's a divorced father of three teenagers residing in North Carolina. He was born in Pasadena, California and currently lives in Eagle Rock. Adam is a professional organizer and aspiring author of social satire. As a soldier he was stationed in Fort Drum, New York and Fort Hood, Texas. He also spent tours in Bosnia, Korea, Kuwait, Baghdad, Baqubah and Mosul. He has been a featured reader with Returning Soldiers Speak, and is a member of the Deadly Writers Platoon at Wellness Works, Glendale.

Wes Cloys, Army Engineer, served in Vietnam from 1965-66. He was married for 32 years to his beautiful wife, Bonnie, who passed away thirteen years ago. He has one son, Adam. For the last four years Wes has volunteered at Wellness Works in many capacities and is a facilitator for the all-around support group at Wellness Works. He is also a facilitator for grief support groups at his church and the Glendale Adventist Hospital. Wes is retired and has made eight trips back to Vietnam over the past seven years. He has been a featured reader with Returning Soldiers Speak, including the 2016 No Ho Lit Crawl and is a member of the Deadly Writers Platoon at Wellness Works, Glendale.

Mary Lu Coughlin is co-founder of Wellness Works with her now deceased friend and business partner Nancy B. Rez, MA, RN. Jean Houston's work, *THE POSSIBLE HUMAN: A Course in Enhancing Your Physical, Mental, and Creative Abilities*, inspired Mary Lu and Mary to begin Wellness Works in 1984. Their vision to provide a welcoming space for people to explore and experience hugs and healing and a taste of personal wholeness within an atmosphere of creativity and professionalism is still alive and well today. Wellness Works is proud to welcome veterans and their families to share in this vision. Mary Lu is excited to begin her journey as a writer.

Eric Fleming, U.S. Army, Desert Storm, Charlie Co., 54th Combat Engineers. After Desert Storm, he drove all the way from the Corn State to the Porn State. Now he writes, practices yoga and martial arts, and hangs out with his cat that sometimes wears pink sunglasses. He has been published in *The Funny Pages* by Judy Brown; *Reader's Digest,* "Laughter is the Best Medicine" and "Animal Jokes, Endangered Species." He has been featured with Returning Soldiers Speak at Beyond Baroque. He is a member of the Deadly Writers Platoon at Wellness Works, Glendale and is currently writing a memoir.

Sandra Squire Fluck, writer, poet, and educator, graduated from U.C.L.A. with a Bachelor of Arts and a Master of Arts in English Literature. She also has a Master of Arts (Religion) from the Lancaster Theological Seminary in Pennsylvania. She has taught English Literature, Creative Writing, English Composition, and Technical Writing in colleges in California and Pennsylvania. She is the founder of bookscover2cover.com, LLC and the senior editor at www.thewritelaunch.com.

Patrick Ignacio's loving parents made him in the Philippines, and he was assembled here in the U.S. of A. He served in the U.S. Marine Corps and did personnel and administration duties, not to mention doing everything else being in a Marine infantry unit. His 13th Marine Expeditionary Unit (Special Operation Capable) liberated Kuwait during Operations Desert Shield/Storm. After being honorably discharged from the Marines he went to college at the University of Southern California and then worked for almost ten years as a caseworker for the American Red Cross. He has contributed articles for the Red Cross Chapter Los Angeles paper and has written Public Service Announcements for the organization. He has been a featured reader with Returning Soldiers Speak, and is a member of the Deadly Writers Platoon at Wellness Works,

Glendale. He is writing a memoir about his service in the Marine Corps so his daughter will understand what it means to serve one's country.

Stephen J. Jacobs, is a U.S. Army veteran, rank E4. He served a 15-month Tour of Duty in Vietnam from 1968-69 in the American Division and 4th Infantry Division. He is a second-generation jazz musician, and a multiple award winning composer, arranger and writer. He is a retired Federal Police Officer and currently CEO, Green Leopard, Inc. and Chui Records and Productions.

Marine Corporal, Kenneth James 0311 Infantry. He served 1½ years with Charlie Co. in the Philippines and with B 1/8 on the U.S.S Incheon and North Carolina. He is the skid row Artist and Poet – and publishes in Everyday Poetry P4 productions. Also google #EscapingSkidRow. He has a Bachelor's in Social Work aspires to get an MFA, and a Ph.D. in Social Justice. His hopes is to continue to help other Veterans with P.T.S.D. and other disabilities. He is always looking to share the spirit of civility through any eclectic and inspired Venues for his art and poetry. Sponsorships would be greatly appreciated and considered. Kenneth has mottos he lives by: "Art for the broader road to civility!" and Love Triumphant amidst adversity! He has won awards for art and poetry, and has shown at the Pasadena Museum of California Art, Riverside Museum of art, and various galleries and other venues. He too, has been featured with Returning Soldiers Speak, and is a member of the Deadly Writers Platoon at Wellness Works, Glendale.

Erren Geraud Kelly comes from a military family. He was stationed in Fort Knox, Kentucky as an Army tanker. His dad was in the Air Force; two uncles served in Vietnam, and his brother fought in two Iraq wars. Erren is a two-time Pushcart nominated poet. His poems have appeared in dozens of print and online publications in the U.S., Canada, and around the world. He is the author of the book *Disturbing The Peace* from Night Ballet Press. Erren received his B.A. in English-Creative Writing from Louisiana State University in Baton Rouge.

Terre Fallon Lindseth, LTC (Ret) served for 27 years. She first enlisted in 1978 at the age of 17 in the Army National Guard. She was commissioned as a 2nd Lieutenant in 1981 and served in the 40th Infantry Division (M) for 14 years. In 1992, and as a company commander, she deployed with her unit to the LA Riots. She transferred to the Army Reserves joining the 425th Civil Affairs Battalion and was deployed on several short missions as a team chief to the Pacific Rim. In 2000 she deployed to Bosnia where she served as Deputy Director of Civil Military Operations in the Tuzla area and was medically retired in 2006 due to injuries sustained while in Bosnia. She has been a featured reader with Returning Soldiers Speak, including the 2016 No Ho Lit Crawl, and is a member of the Deadly Writers Platoon at Wellness Works, Glendale. She is happily married.

Dallas Dorsett Mathers, graphic designer and screenwriter, is the daughter of a WWII veteran, the widow of a cold war veteran and the sister of a Viet Nam War veteran. She has great respect for those who serve the country in the military, and is very happy to have participated in this worthy and meaningful project. She is founder of The Studio City Writers Group.

Lisa Raggio currently serves as the Executive Director of Wellness Works, a service provider for veterans in Glendale, and is the Chair and co-founder of the Veterans Coalition of Glendale and the Verdugos, established in 2012. In addition, she is the Vice President of Veterans Services for Leadership Pasadena; a member of the Veterans Advisory Committee for Congressmember Cardenas of the 29th district; and is a member of Intelecom Learning, Community College Student Veterans Advisory Committee, and she co-founded and co-chairs the Veterans Education Assistance Fund serving local student Veterans. Lisa created the YWCA of Glendale's "Focus on Female Veterans" program launched in 2012, recognized as a "Best Practice" program in the 2014 California Department of Veterans Affairs' Women Veterans Outreach Toolkit. Furthermore, she is honored to have been nominated for the following regarding her work serving veterans: the James Irvine Foundation's Leadership award; the national YWCA USA Advocacy Award, and she has been a VIP guest of the White House and First Lady for a "Champions of Change" event representing the national YWCA.

She is a proud and privileged granddaughter, sister, sister-in-law, and niece of service members from World War I to post 9/11 who believes that serving veterans is her "vocation."

Glenn Schiffman was a Conscientious Objector during the Vietnam War. He has a BA, an MFA, and an MSC, and is a writer and respected Elder in the Native American community. His writing credits include: Writer/Producer CD-ROM and laser disc IBM's Eduquest Group of the book *Black Elk Speaks* (1990); Writer on the Eduquest publication of *The Declaration of Independence* (1991); Writer of historical essays and literary reviews Salem Press, McGill Annual Literary Review, Newbury Library (1990-1995); Writer, Associate Producer of the *Mystic Fire* documentary celebrating the release of wolves into Yellowstone National Park (1994); and was one of four finalists (out of 2700 entrants) in the Next Top Spiritual Author competition (Hyperion Press) in 2010. He self-published *The Way I Was Taught* (March 2014), and has conducted readings from it before Home Boys Industries, the Joseph Campbell Roundtable, Pasadena IONS Chapter, and New Roads School. *The Way I Was Taught* reached #1 in its genre on Amazon. Glenn has been a featured reader with Returning Soldiers Speak, including the 2016 No Ho Lit Crawl.

Leilani Squire was born at Tripler Army Hospital in Honolulu while her father, Grant R. Squire, was deployed on an aircraft carrier off the coast of Okinawa during the Korean War. She is a writer, a certified creativity coach, and has been working with veterans and their families for over 7 years to help them tell their stories. She has taught at the West Los Angeles VA Domiciliary, Wellness Works, Glendale, Mil-Tree in Joshua Tree and online at bookscover2cover. She is founder and director of Returning Soldiers Speak and senior editor of *Returning Soldiers Speak: An Anthology of Prose and Poetry by Soldiers and Veterans* and the Poetry Editor for the online literary journal established by poet Paul Hellwig, *Vietnam War Poetry*. She is the facilitator and a member of the Deadly Writers Platoon, and spearheaded the arts project of *The Storytellers: Veterans and Family Members Write About Military Life*.

Roger (Rick) Thurnell. Sgt. U.S.A.F., Miss. Guid. and Ctrl. Spclst. Served 1969-73, the last four years of Nam. Following his separation from the Air Force, he worked temporary jobs and intermittent stints in college. For many years he was a professional driver, a counselor for 7 years, a massage therapist for 5 years and practiced various other healing endeavors. For decades, his true passion has been delving into humanity's beginnings. He has been a featured historical research reader with Returning Soldiers Speak and is a member of the Deadly Writers Platoon at Wellness Works, Glendale.

Denise M. Woodard is the *nom de plume* of a veteran who wishes to remain anonymous.

With our deepest gratitude ...

Thank you!!!

CPSIA information can be obtained
at www.ICGtesting.com
Printed in the USA
LVHW011215101119
636879LV00012B/932